# Bullying in our Society

Series Editor: Cara Acred

Volume 232

Independence Educational Publishers

First published by Independence Educational Publishers

The Studio, High Green

Great Shelford

Cambridge CB22 5EG

England

© Independence 2012

## Copyright

## Photocopy licence

## British Library Cataloguing in Publication Data

Bullying in our society. – (Issues ; v. 232)

1. Bullying.

I. Series II. Acred, Cara.

302.3'43-dc23

ISBN-13: 9781 86168 625 1

## Printed in Great Britain

MWL Print Group Ltd

# Contents

# Introduction

**Bullying in our Society** is Volume 232 in the 'Issues' series. The aim of the series is to offer current, diverse information about important issues in our world, from a UK perspective.

## ABOUT BULLYING IN OUR SOCIETY

Did you know that on a daily basis, an average of 160,000 children miss school because they fear they will be bullied if they attend classes? Bullying is not always physical, but can be psychological too, and can occur at home, in schools and in the workplace. This is especially true with the rise of technology; cyberbullying and trolling are now becoming a major concern, with incidents of harassment via Facebook and Twitter as well as 'sexting' on the increase. This book looks at the forms that bullying can take and the spread of cyberbullying, with information on how bullying affects victims and how it can be tackled.

## OUR SOURCES

Titles in the *Issues* series are designed to function as educational resource books, providing a balanced overview of a specific subject.

The information in our books is comprised of facts, articles and opinions from many different sources, including:

- Newspaper reports and opinion pieces
- Website fact sheets
- Magazine and journal articles
- Statistics and surveys
- Government reports
- Literature from special interest groups

## A NOTE ON CRITICAL EVALUATION

Because the information reprinted here is from a number of different sources, readers should bear in mind the origin of the text and whether the source is likely to have a particular bias when presenting information (or when conducting their research). It is hoped that, as you read about the many aspects of the issues explored in this book, you will critically evaluate the information presented.

It is important that you decide whether you are being presented with facts or opinions. Does the writer give a biased or unbiased report? If an opinion is being expressed, do you agree with the writer? Is there potential bias to the 'facts' or statistics behind an article?

## ASSIGNMENTS

In the back of this book, you will find a selection of assignments designed to help you engage with the articles you have been reading and to explore your own opinions. Some tasks will take longer than others and there is a mixture of design, writing and research based activities that you can complete alone or in a group.

## FURTHER RESEARCH

At the end of each article we have listed its source and a website that you can visit if you would like to conduct your own research. Please remember to critically evaluate any sources that you consult and consider whether the information you are viewing is accurate and unbiased.

# Bullying

*Information from Women's and Children's Health Network.*

**B**ullying is when hurtful or upsetting things are repeatedly said or done to people. Bullying is also called harassment or peer abuse.

⇨ It can involve physical violence such as hitting, kicking, punching, pushing or verbal violence including teasing and name-calling.

⇨ It can also include damaging, stealing or hiding a victim's things or making demands for money or favours.

⇨ Another form is to exclude victims, by encouraging others not to have anything to do with them, spreading lies or stories about them, ignoring them and not speaking to them.

⇨ Another type of harassment is cyberbullying. Cyberbullying uses technology to harass, embarrass or threaten to hurt someone physically

Bullying is a form of violence and a way of having power over others. It needs to be taken seriously as it can have long-term effects on the child being bullied, the one doing the bullying and those who witness it.

Bullying often happens in places where children spend lots of time, such as in families, early childhood centres, schools, sporting or recreational clubs and work places. Any organisation which has contact with children is required to have policies to keep them safe. However children can be bullied anywhere and it's not always by other children – adults can be bullies too. Cyber bullying has become a real concern because it can happen anywhere at any time, even in the safety of your home.

Sometimes children find it hard to talk about being bullied but will show it in their behaviour. They need adults to listen, believe and support them. You can help them by talking to adults with the power to stop it. You can also help children to develop coping strategies and to take action themselves. This way they can gain a sense of control and feel more confident.

## What is bullying?

Bullying can include threatening, teasing, name-calling, gossiping and spreading rumours, ignoring or not letting people be part of a group (excluding), ganging up, playing cruel jokes, preventing others from going where they want to, or taking away their belongings. It can also be pushing, shoving or hitting and other forms of physical abuse.

Bullying is not about a conflict that needs to be worked out; it's about one person or group trying to have power over others. It's important to develop a long-term approach which stops bullying at the source and permanently, rather than just blocking one avenue of contact. If bullying becomes assault, discrimination or harassment it's breaking the law and you may need to involve the police.

It's important that all children learn bullying is not okay and can be stopped. They need to know they can play an important role in stopping bullying by telling responsible adults who can do something about it.

⇨ A child who is being bullied needs to see that things can be done so they don't feel unable to protect themselves in the future.

⇨ Children who witness bullying can be traumatised by the experience and require support as well.

⇨ Children who bully others need to learn how to develop different skills so this behaviour doesn't limit them in adult life.

## Where does it happen?

Places where children and young people spend lots of time is where bullying happens most, including families. Parents can bully children, and siblings can bully each other. With the increase in blended families there's often children across a broad age range living in the same household. This creates power differences between siblings which can set the scene for bullying.

Studies show that one in six Australian school students are bullied every week. These students are three times more likely to become depressed. Children can be bullied in classrooms, gyms and toilet blocks, in the school grounds or whilst getting to or from school. All early childhood centres and schools in South Australia have a responsibility to protect children from bullying.

Sporting clubs, recreational and interest groups are other places where children are at risk of being bullied. In sporting clubs, bullying can occur on or off the pitch and can involve players, parents, coaches, umpires or spectators. It can be quite common to hear parents and spectators at children's sporting events yelling out hurtful or negative comments from the sidelines.

Sometimes it's a coach using 'put-downs' to motivate players. Most sporting clubs have Member Protection Policies which address harassment, discrimination and abuse, as well as a complaints process. As organisations which involve children they're also required to have ways to protect them.

## Cyberbullying

Technology has increased the ways bullying can happen.

⇨ Mobile phones, emails, websites, chat rooms, social networking sites or instant messaging can be used to bully others.

⇨ Cyberbullying can include repeated teasing, sending nasty or threatening messages, damaging information or photos.

⇨ It's against the law to threaten someone this way.

⇨ Cyberbullying can be very scary because it can happen any time of the day or night. It can feel like there's no way to get away from it, even in the safety of your own home.

A cyberbully might be someone your child knows, but messages can be sent without knowing who they are from. Your child may be worried you'll take their phone or email address away if you know they're being bullied. It's important though for everyone that they don't keep bullying a secret.

## Children who bully

Children who bully can:

⇨ Be very self-focused and not good at controlling their impulses and aggression

⇨ Have limited self-awareness and take little responsibility for their actions

⇨ Need power over others to feel important, admired and accepted. This often makes up for feeling scared, alone or not in control in other areas of their life

⇨ Think that bullying makes them popular or cool

⇨ Want to win at all cost. They don't pick on children who will stand up to them, they pick on children they know they can intimidate

⇨ See bullying as fun and believe some kinds of people deserve to be bullied, e.g. because of how they look or because they're from a certain group

⇨ Be easily influenced by aggressive 'models' (in real life and in movies)

⇨ Come from a violent family background and be the victims of bullying themselves

⇨ Have had extreme discipline, or sometimes limited discipline

⇨ Bully others as pay-back for some 'unfair' treatment.

Children who bully might be outgoing and do it in front of others so they can get recognition. Sometimes they're part of popular groups. Or they might be more reserved, controlling and manipulating others in subtle ways.

⇨ They're not usually affected by the distress of the victim and are likely to go on hurting others if they're not stopped.

⇨ They often don't do well at school and can have trouble with the law as they get older.

⇨ As adults they're more likely to bully their partners, their own children and people at work.

Bullying is a learned behaviour which means children who bully are able to learn different ways of dealing with things. It's important though to not bully the bully so that children don't get a double message.

## Children who are bullied

Any child can be bullied. Sometimes children who are popular, very good at something, or who are very smart or attractive can be victims of bullying. However, bullies most often pick on children who seem easy to hurt. Children who are picked on can often be:

⇨ Different in some way, including their physical appearance, having a disability, being from a different cultural group or not fitting in with gender stereotypes

⇨ Anxious or stressed, lacking confidence to stand up for themselves

⇨ Not good at sport or find schoolwork difficult

⇨ Shy and keep to themselves, or find it hard to socialise with other children

⇨ Younger, smaller or not as strong and therefore unable to 'fight back'.

## Children who witness bullying

Children who witness bullying may be traumatised by the experience. They may feel powerless to stop someone else getting hurt. They need to talk about their feelings and learn what they can do.

It's important for all children to understand that bullying isn't okay, even if they're not involved. They can play a part in stopping it by:

⇨ telling a responsible adult such as a parent, a teacher or coach

⇨ refusing to join in and ignoring the bully

⇨ walking up to the person being bullied, talking to them and going with them to get support

⇨ making friends with children new to a school or club.

## Signs of being bullied

Children may not always tell adults they're being bullied. They may be afraid or ashamed, think it's their fault or that it's 'dobbing' to tell someone. They may have been threatened with something worse if they tell. They might show some of the following:

⇨ Bruises, scratches or torn clothing

⇨ Damage or loss of personal belongings

⇨ Sleeping problems, e.g. not sleeping, nightmares, bed wetting

⇨ Changes in behaviour such as being withdrawn or teary

⇨ Loss of confidence

⇨ Not doing well at school

⇨ Talking about problems at the place they're being bullied, or trying to avoid going there

⇨ Finding excuses to not go, e.g. feeling sick

⇨ Wanting to change the way they usually get there

⇨ Being upset after going to the venue

⇨ Saying they don't have any friends or they hate other children there

⇨ Not wanting to talk about their day.

These signs don't always mean your child is being bullied, but you need to check out what's worrying them.

## The effects of bullying

Bullying can make children feel afraid, lonely, embarrassed, angry, upset or physically ill. If it's not stopped it can affect health and well-being into adult life. Children who are bullied can have a higher risk of mental health problems such as anxiety, stress, low self-esteem or depression.

Bullied children learn to be 'on guard' all the time, checking where the bully is and wondering when it will happen again. When children are 'on alert' like this, they're less able to concentrate or learn. Their friendships may suffer as they're often tense, worried and unable to have fun. They may begin to believe they deserve it and become withdrawn, isolated and feel less able to fit into their world. They can even think about suicide.

Children who are being bullied need to know they have options.

⇨ A younger child may not be able to physically protect themselves, but they can let an adult know who can do something about it.

⇨ An older child may need support to think through the things they could do themselves.

Be very careful they don't think being bullied is their fault. Even though they can do things to feel more confident, it's the bully who needs to change and stop the behaviour.

## What you can do

It's not always easy for a parent to know when and how to step in. The child's age, maturity and safety all need to be considered.

⇨ Listen to your child and take seriously his feelings and fears

⇨ Don't call him names e.g. 'weak' or 'a sook' and don't let anyone else do so

⇨ Make sure he's safe. Sometimes this may require taking action he's not happy with

⇨ Try to give him as much power as possible to find solutions so he can feel more in control. Solving problems himself, with your support, can create a real increase in self-esteem

⇨ Work on improving his confidence by building on the things he does well

⇨ If he's been traumatised he may need professional help.

Stop bullying where it's happening:

⇨ Meet with the school or organisation where the bullying is happening and ask about their policy and procedures for dealing with bullying

⇨ Make a list of the things that have happened. Be clear and firm about the impact of the bullying and the need for them to stop it. Find out what steps the school or club will take to prevent it happening again

⇨ Be prepared to name the children who bully. If bullying persists, write down who, what, where and when

⇨ Keep in contact until the problem is sorted out. If you find it difficult to be assertive, take another adult with you for support.

If it's cyberbullying:

⇨ Let children know they need to be open with you so you can make sure they're safe online

⇨ Be careful who knows phone numbers and email addresses. You may need to change phone numbers and email addresses in the short-term, but remember you need to take actions which stop bullying permanently

⇨ Contact your phone and Internet providers to see what can be done to prevent calls or remove bullying material

⇨ Talk to the school principal if cyberbullying involves students from school

⇨ Report cyberbullying to the police if it doesn't stop.

## How you can help children

Help her work out ways to deal with bullying and to feel good about herself. This could include:

⇨ Talking to an adult who can do something to stop the bullying, e.g. a teacher, a coach, a group leader

⇨ Ignoring the bully and walking away

⇨ Practising being confident when not in the situation so she knows how to react when it's happening

⇨ Not getting emotional, e.g. staying calm so the bully doesn't win by getting her to react

⇨ Not getting physical which can end up in being hurt or getting blamed for the bully's actions

⇨ Being true to herself, focussing on her strengths and building these up

⇨ Making new friends and doing things together.

## What might be done at school

There are six major approaches listed in a book by Professor Ken Rigby:

1. **The traditional disciplinary approach** – punishment or consquences.

2. **Strengthening the victim** – the person being targeted is instructed or trained so as to cope more effectively with the bullying.

3. **Mediation** – individuals involved meet with a trained mediator to explore ways of resolving the situation.

4. **Restorative practice** – at a meeting the bully/bullies must listen to how the 'target' feels, reflect on what is happening, and act restoratively (e.g. by making an acceptable apology).

5. **The support group method** – the target(s) are interviewed and an acccount of their distress is communicated to the bullies at a meeting where other support students are present. The people at the meeting work out how they will help resolve the problem.

6. **The method of shared concern** – a practitioner meets separately with the students being bullied, then with those who are doing the bullying – then gets them together to develop a plan to resolve the problem.

*Rigby K, 'Bullying intervention in school: six major approaches' ACER 2010 (www.kenrigby.net)*

## Reminders

⇨ Take action if needed to keep your child safe

⇨ Let all children know bullying is wrong and to tell an adult who can do something about it

⇨ Take their fears and feelings seriously. It's normal to feel embarrassed, scared or hurt if you're being bullied

⇨ Reassure him that being bullied is not his fault and that he's not alone

⇨ Help him work out his own ways of dealing with bullying so he feels he has some control

⇨ Help him feel good about other things in his life

⇨ Stop bullying at the source and permanently. Involve the school or club or wherever it's a happening. Don't give up until it stops

⇨ Get professional support if bullying happens a lot in different situations and with different children.

⇨ The above information is reprinted with kind permission from Women's and Children's Health Network. Visit their website www.wchn.sa.gov.au for more information.

# Bullying statistics

***Information from BullyingMatters.***

44% of suicides among ten- to 14-year-olds may be bullying-related.

⇨ The Office of National Statistics had recorded 176 cases of suicides of 10-to-14-year olds between 2000 and 2008 in England, Scotland and Wales.

⇨ Over 20% of kids admit to being a bully or participating in bully-like activities.

⇨ Over one half of bullying & Cyber-Bullying events go unreported to authorities or parents.

⇨ In 2009 surveys showed over 100,000 children carried guns to school as a result of being bullied.

⇨ 28% of students who carry weapons in school have witnessed violence in their homes.

⇨ On a daily average 160,000 children miss school because they fear they will be bullied if they attend classes.

⇨ On a monthly average 282,000 students are physically attacked by a bully each month.

⇨ Every seven minutes a child is bullied on a school playground.

⇨ 46% of males and 26% of females admit to having been involved in physical fights as a result of being bullied.

⇨ Over 85% of our teenagers say that revenge as an aftermath of being bullied is the leading cause for school shootings and homicide.

⇨ A child commits suicide as a direct result of being bullied once every half hour with 19,000 bullied children attempting to commit suicide over the course of one year.

⇨ Over 75% of our students are subjected to harassment by a bully or Cyber-Bully and experience physical, psychological and/or emotional abuse.

⇨ The above information is reprinted with kind permission from BullyingMatters. Visit their website www.bullying-matters.co.uk for more information.

# As Kate Middleton knows, girls make the best bullies

**Kate Middleton's grim experience at school strikes a chord with Cassandra Jardine, who was also ostracised by her female peers.**

*By Cassandra Jardine*

Kate Middleton should have had an easy time of it at boarding school. Her parents hadn't set her up to be teased by giving her red hair, spots, poor eyesight or a silly name. She was pretty, leggy, clever and good at hockey when she arrived at Downe House, aged 13.

Yet other girls soon made her life a misery. She had books knocked out of her hands, was pushed to the back of the lunch queue and no one wanted to eat with her, according to Jessica Hay, a friend from her next school.

How much Hay's memories can be trusted, 16 years on, is debatable: she spoke of faeces placed in Middleton's bed – unlikely given she was a day girl. What isn't under dispute is that the royal soon-to-be-weds have chosen the charity Beatbullying as a beneficiary of their wedding.

Kate may not wish to discuss it, but the experience of bullying is virtually universal. 81 per cent of school students say they have been bullied, according to Beatbullying. In the celebrity world, a touch of bullying is almost a requirement on the CV, whether you are an adventurer such as Sir Ranulph Fiennes – tormented at Eton for being too pretty – or an actress like Kate Winslet who was given hell at her state school in Reading for being fat.

It often suits the celebrity backstory to play the ugly duckling turned into swan, but there's no need to stand out from the crowd in order to be a victim. Like Kate Middleton, I was ostracised for two terms at the end of primary school, not because there was anything especially peculiar about me – as far as I know – but because a classmate's parents were getting a divorce and she felt like offloading her distress onto someone else.

Those two terms felt like an eternity. While everyone else chatted and played, I cut ever-larger holes in my school uniform, hoping my mother would notice that it wasn't moths at work. It took her a long time to spot my misery. So I have every sympathy with Kate Middleton whose only 'crime' as far as anonymous contemporaries can recall was to be a 'non-entity'. Most likely she was picked upon because she was a day girl among boarders, who joined at the age of 13.

Newcomers weren't welcome, as another girl found when she moved from a London day school to join what could have been Kate's year at Downe House for the Sixth Form. 'At Downe House I found the girls blindingly clone-like. "You mean you didn't go to Cornwall?" they said when I told them where I had been on holiday.' She left Downe House after a matter of weeks. 'They couldn't understand anyone being different. Bullying has nothing to do with the victim being inferior, it's to do with the bullies being scared.'

The revelations have done no favours to the reputations of either single sex or boarding schools. 'People assume that bullying is related to socio-economic class, but masses of bullying goes on in the leafy suburbs,' says psychologist Michael Eslea. 'When Childline started a special boarding school helpline in the 1990s, they were inundated with calls.'

Analysis of bullying dynamics has become more sophisticated since then. The victim and the bully are no

longer considered to be the only players, says Eslea. 'Bullying is seen as a peer process: bystanders are just as much of a problem. There's a big emphasis on trying to turn bystanders into defenders of the victim.'

Every school now has an anti-bullying policy, but the tormenting goes on because, as Downe's ex-head Susan Cameron says, it is a way of 'working out the pecking order'. Boys do still tend to lose their tempers, fight, and then forget their differences. Girls more often operate sly longer-term campaigns, often using social network sites. I've seen that pattern with my own children (two boys, three girls) and the inter-girl fights are far more poisonous.

Bullying, however, still accounts for around ten children's suicides a year. Beatbullying's approach is to get the children in a school on side as mentors. 'They are the ones able to change the culture,' says deputy CEO Richard Piggin.

In my experience the presence of the opposite sex generally has a moderating influence on bad behaviour, but *The Good Schools Guide*'s senior editor Jeanette Wallis says there is no difference between single sex and co-ed schools: 'We see as many parents wishing to change schools because their children have been bullied at co-ed schools as at single sex.'

Changing schools may give children the feeling that problems can be avoided not faced. The key, says educational psychologist Elaine Douglas, is 'acting as if', so however miserable the victim feels she should act as if she has all the confidence in the world. Another strategy is to find someone else on the sidelines and befriend that girl (or boy). Being ignored is often the most difficult situation to deal with because teachers can't punish assailants, and even a witty victim can't answer back nonchalantly if no one is listening. But facing down bullies takes maturity so there is much to be said, too, for turning to a helpline. Respondents generally add in a much needed ego-boost while they are dispensing advice.

When Kate Middleton was having a miserable time at Downe House, no such helpline was available. Michael and Carole Middleton clearly felt that the only way they could make life happier for their eldest child was to remove her from the school. There is a risk that the situation may repeat itself at the next school unless the child has learned something from the experience.

Maybe she had. Kate probably settled in well at Marlborough College because the girls, among them Jessica Hay, were briefed that the thin, shy girl joining them mid-year needed looking after as she had had a bad time.

Marlborough could justifiably claim to have been the making of our new Princess because she left school equipped with many friends and A-level grades good enough for St Andrew's, where she knew Prince William could be found.

But perhaps the true making of her was at Downe House. There's nothing like having a bad time for adding a touch of steel to a personality. After being ostracised at school, I made sure it didn't happen again by making as many friends as possible at my next school.

Kate did rather better from her formative bad experience. If, 16 years ago, she decided to pay back those who thought she was a non-entity, she has certainly succeeded.

*5 April 2011*

⇨ The above article originally appeared in *The Telegraph*. Visit their website www.telegraph.co.uk for more information.

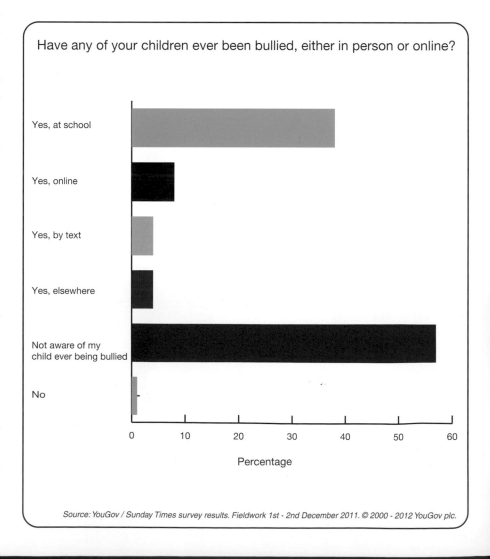

Have any of your children ever been bullied, either in person or online?

# Teasing, taunts and threats: school-children are waging 'psychological warfare' on the nation's playing fields

**Children as young as eight are victims of mental and physical bullying on the school playing field, according to research published today by Marylebone Cricket Club (MCC) and Chance to Shine.**

As schools return from the Easter break, many pupils will view their summer games lessons and matches with trepidation. Two-thirds (66%) of 1,010 parents of children aged eight to 16 polled say they witness different forms of mental intimidation while watching their children play sport. Teasing (43%), swearing (40%), taunts (34%) and verbal threats (16%) are common tactics of the sports bullies.

More than two-fifths of parents (42%) say their child lost confidence after being bullied on the playing field, a fifth feel their child was reluctant to take part in sport as a result of the mind games; while one in ten parents reports that their child gave up at least one sport entirely as a result.

In a separate survey of 1,250 children, aged eight to 16, 68% say they, too, see verbal abuse during school matches and over half (51%) admit to being a victim of teasing, taunts and threats on the sports field. The majority (55%) also witness physical violence, with a quarter of children seeing a team-mate deliberately tripped, kicked or pushed over.

To help teach young people how to play matches in a competitive but sporting manner, MCC and Chance to Shine are delivering a nationwide scheme to encourage 'fair play' in schools. From today, Chance to Shine coaches will deliver assemblies and lessons in good sportsmanship to around half a million children in 4,000 state schools, as part of the MCC Spirit of Cricket scheme.

According to the research, three fifths of children feel unable to tell anyone about the bullying. Asked 'why not?', a number of children say they were 'too scared' or that there was 'no point'. As one 12-year-old explains: 'At secondary school you need to sort out your own problems sometimes since your parents cannot do anything about it and the coaches and teachers are often very busy.'

Dads are more likely to notice the mind games when children play sport, but mums are more likely to take action when they witness it. Mums are far more likely than dads to take the issue up with the teacher or coach; whereas dads are more likely to confront the bully themselves. A third of parents (34%) witness another parent upsetting children involved in a game or match.

It wasn't all bad news, as the image of the stereotypical sadistic sports teacher seems to be on the decline. Two-fifths of parents recall how they were teased, taunted and verbally undermined by their PE teacher or coach when they were at school. Today, however, more than two-thirds of children (67%) polled say they had never seen this kind of behaviour by staff.

John Stephenson, Head of Cricket at MCC says, 'The results from the survey highlight an alarming trend in school sport, which needs to be proactively addressed. MCC's ongoing partnership with Chance to Shine provides the perfect vehicle to do this, as children get the opportunity to learn about the MCC Spirit of Cricket principles of playing hard, but fair.'

Wasim Khan, Chief Executive of Chance to Shine adds, 'It is worrying to hear that this kind of psychological warfare is being waged on our school playing fields. We are teaching children from a young age to play competitively, but to respect the opposition as well as their team-mates. We need to stamp out this bullying in school sport.'

Other highlights of the MCC/Chance to Shine survey include:

⇨ Belfast, Birmingham, Cardiff and Liverpool are the cities most affected by mental intimidation by children on the school sports field according to parents in the regions;

⇨ 16% of children admit getting their own back on the bully;

⇨ Almost one in five children say their team-mates and opposition have little to no respect for officials on the field of play;

⇨ Nearly half of children admit that they like their favourite sports stars less when they see them name-calling, swearing and insulting other players. One in five say they stop liking them entirely;

⇨ Wayne Rooney is rated the worst role model for children (18%), closely followed by John Terry (17%). Dads feel the Chelsea skipper sets the worst example to their kids.

⇨ Information from Chance to Shine. Visit their website www.chancetoshine.org for more information.

# Victims of bullying

## Information from the Department for Education.

**B**ullying pervasiveness and frequency is heightened amongst certain groups. But bullying is a significant problem amongst all young people.

In 2010 Beatbullying carried out analysis of two research data sets to explore the characteristics of persistent bullying. The study suggests that the characteristics that drive persistent bullying are less likely to be members of a particularly vulnerable group and more likely to be about 'any difference' (*Persistency, Duration and Vulnerable Groups*, Beatbullying, 2010).

What are the drivers of persistent bullying?

⇨ 40% 'looks'

⇨ 25% 'because good at something'

⇨ 10% race

⇨ 8% SEN/Health

⇨ 5% religion

⇨ 3% sexuality

## Characteristics of bullying victims

Regular victims of bullying tend to have common characteristics, one is 'passive' or 'submissive', characterised by (Olweus, 1991):

⇨ Tendency to be anxious and insecure

⇨ Low self-esteem, with a negative valuation of themselves

⇨ Few friends; with the friends they are likely to have being low social status themselves

⇨ An aversion to using violence, meaning they are unlikely to retaliate

⇨ Amongst boys, they are also characterised by a relative physical weakness

⇨ Many of the above characteristics likely to be both a cause and effect of bullying.

The other far less common category is 'provocative victims'. Olweus reported that fewer than one in five victims are 'provocative' (Olweus, 1984). Provocative victims have a mix of anxious and aggressive behaviour patterns, coupled with poor concentration.

⇨ Behaviour can provoke groups of people, rather than just individuals

⇨ Mencap suggest that learning difficulties leading to poor social skills could result in 'provacative victim' behaviour (Mencap, 2007).

## What is the impact of bullying?

There is much evidence of bullying causing long-term psychological damage.

In broad terms, we know that children worry about bullying:

⇨ 25% of young people say they 'most worry about bullying'

⇨ 20% of children on *StayingSafe* say they worry about bullying (*StayingSafe*, DCSF, 2009).

Many children are not concerned about bullying, and 38% of children think that bullying is a 'part of growing up' (*StayingSafe*, DCSF, 2009).

### Impact on achievement

LSYPE findings at a total surveyed level suggest that bullying is 'associated' with lowered Key Stage 4 achievement (*Characteristics of Bullying Victims in Schools*, DfE, 2010).

Whilst these findings do not demonstrate that bullying causes lowered achievement, the authors of the report note that 'the bullying has been shown to occur earlier in time than the educational outcome. It is entirely possible that both bullying and educational outcomes have common antecedents, but we have

tested for this as far as possible in our analyses' (*Characteristics of Bullying Victims in Schools*, DfE, 2010).

⇨ Young people who had been bullied had a significantly lower Key Stage 4 score than those who hadn't been bullied.

⇨ On average, young people who had been bullied had a Key Stage 4 score 13 points lower than those who hadn't been bullied. This is the equivalent of two GCSE grades.

⇨ The type of bullying that affected school attainment the most was taking money or possessions.

### Impact on well-being

Beatbullying research into persistency and impact gives a personally reported perspective on the impact of bullying. This also draws conclusions about the more serious effect of persistent bullying compared to isolated bullying (*Persistency, Duration and Vulnerable Groups*, Beatbullying, 2010):

⇨ 15% of those children who were persistently bullied said they thought about killing themselves.

⇨ 22% of children persistently bullied said bullying made them give up their interests compared to 7% who experienced isolated bullying.

⇨ 25% of persistently bullied children said they changed their personality compared to just 17% who were bullied in isolation.

⇨ 15% of persistently bullied children said they self-harmed – a figure five times higher than that recorded for children bullied who stated they were bullied occasionally in the same research.

⇨ Information from the Department of Education. Visit their website www.education.gov.uk for more information.

# University discovers link between bullying, self-harm and suicide

**Both bullies and their victims have been found to be three times more likely to consider suicide or actions of self-harm by the age of 11, according to recent research conducted by Warwick University.**

*By Jack Shardlow*

In the recent paper published in the *Journal of the American Academy of Child and Adolescent Psychiatry*, researchers believe that they have found that involvement in bullying greatly increases the chances of a child self-harming or contemplating suicide. The authors of the paper, Catherine Winsper, Tanya Lereya and Dieter Wolke, are all based at Warwick University.

The subjects of the research were 6,034 children whose mothers had enrolled in the 'Children of the 90s', a long-term health research study at the University of Bristol. The research carried out at Warwick aimed towards the discovery of the levels of bullying in children, as well as investigating how prevalent thoughts of self-harm and suicide were in 11-and-12-year-old children.

After collecting information from parents, teachers and the children involved, the research concluded that the increase in suicidal thoughts could not be attributed to factors other than the involvement in bullying.

When compared with children who have never been bullied, the victims of bullying were found to be three times more likely to contemplate suicide or self-harm, while long-term victims of bullying were found to be six times more likely.

The research also found that the children responsible for the bullying were at a raised risk of suicidal thoughts and self-harming behaviour.

Wolke, based in the Department of Psychology and Warwick Medical School, said that '4.8 per cent of this community population reported suicidal thoughts and 4.6 per cent reported suicidal or self-injurious behaviour.'

He explained how the study shows that 'health practitioners should be aware of the relationship between bullying and suicide', since very real risks appear to be evident much earlier than expected.

The report calls for 'intervention schemes from primary school onwards', believing that primary schools, could and should be doing more.'

Suicide is a leading cause of death in the UK; in 2008 there were 4,282 recorded suicides in England alone. Men between the ages of 15 and 24 are at a particularly high risk.

Izzy John, the Students' Union (SU) Welfare Officer, said that 'people look at bullying and think it is just something that happens at school, but actually it does happen at university level as well'.

She explained how it is often supposed that 'there is an expectation on people to put up with what they simply shouldn't have to.' Too often bullying is dismissed as something that happens amongst children and that is 'just a part of growing up'.

There is a range of support systems in place for any students who believe that they have been, or are being bullied at the University. For students who are suffering from bullying in their halls of residence, the first port of call should be their Resident Tutor; for other students there is the Student Support Services located in the SU.

*12 March 2012*

⇨ The above information is reprinted with kind permission from *The Boar* – The University of Warwick Students' Newspaper. Visit their website www.theboar.org for more information.

# Racist bullying

*The following information from the Anti-Bullying Network gives an overview of racist bullying issues.*

### What is racist bullying?

Racist violence, harassment and abuse are closely related to, and sometimes difficult to distinguish from, bullying. Racist bullying in schools can range from ill-considered remarks, which are not intended to be hurtful, to deliberate physical attacks causing serious injury.

Racist bullying can be identified by the motivation of the bully, the language used, and/or by the fact that victims are singled out because of the colour of their skin, the way they talk, their ethnic grouping or by their religious or cultural practices.

In most contexts, it is mainly people from black and minority ethnic communities who are subjected to racism, but concern has also been expressed about prejudice against other groups including English people and travellers.

The word 'bigotry' is often used to describe the attitude of some sections of the population towards members of certain religious faiths, e.g. those with Roman Catholic or Protestant beliefs. This may also be the trigger for some incidents of bullying in schools.

### Is racist bullying a problem in schools?

Racist bullying in schools can be a problem in two ways:

Children who experience it have their education disrupted. They may be unable to concentrate on lessons because of feelings of fear or anger. Their self-confidence may be damaged and, as a result, they may never fulfil their potential.

Schools that ignore it, or deny its existence, give the wrong message to young people. The success of our multi-cultural society depends upon the children of today growing up to be adults who are prepared to speak out against racism.

### What can schools do?

Many schools, particularly those in areas where there are large ethnic minority populations, have well-developed policies on multi-cultural and anti-racist education.

They have clear procedures for dealing with racist incidents, and the curriculum covers the knowledge, skills and values which children need to tackle racism when they meet it and to help them to become adults who respect different cultures.

However, there are also schools where there are few or no children from ethnic minorities and where little has been done to address racism. In such situations, while it may be true that there are few overtly racist incidents, racist attitudes can flourish if left unchecked.

As a first step schools may need to embark on an awareness-raising exercise.

### Should racist bullying be treated differently from other types of bullying?

Racism is a very serious problem that has the potential to destroy communities. It deserves its own response in schools. We cannot assume that every school which has an anti-bullying policy will deal effectively with all the issues relating to racism.

Racist bullying must be explicitly discussed in the classroom and there must be clear guidelines for dealing with incidents.

### In the classroom

The work which schools do to tackle bullying can also be effective in reducing racism, child abuse and other related issues. Children can learn skills, such as assertiveness and empathising; they can acquire knowledge about relationships, rights and responsibilities; and they can develop values such as openness and respecting difference.

However, this learning will only be effective if the context in which it can be used is specifically discussed. If young people learn that a skill like assertiveness can be useful in tackling, say, child abuse they will not necessarily assume that it can be used in other situations in which they find themselves, such as racist bullying.

With regard to knowledge, they may not realise that some words which are in common use are perceived as being racist by black or Asian pupils unless this is openly discussed in the classroom.

### Dealing with incidents

Racist bullying cannot be tolerated in schools. Guidelines are needed to help schools deal with racism. These should describe appropriate responses and they should cover bullying by, and of, all members of the school community – adult and children.

Some local authorities have issued schools with such guidelines. A common piece of advice is to monitor and record all racist incidents. Beyond this they usually list possible responses, which might range from a simple reprimand to exclusion or a referral to the police.

Some schools have combined their anti-racist and anti-bullying guidelines. Such a unifying exercise is not easy but it should help schools to cope with the many demands made upon them and to provide a rational and consistent response to bullying of all kinds.

⇨ The above information is reproduced with kind permission from Ealing Grid for Learning. Visit their website www.egfl.org.uk for more information.

*© 2012 Ealing*

# Advice to resolve racist bullying

**Britain is a multi-racial and multi-faith country and everyone has the right to have their culture and religion respected by others.**

Nobody has the right to call you names or to treat you badly because of your colour, race or religion. It's illegal and it can be stopped. You don't have to be a different colour to suffer racist bullying. You might have come from Romania or the former Yugoslavia.

Neither is racist bullying confined to colour of skin. We've had complaints of non-Welsh and non-Scots children experiencing bullying in those countries. Other complaints have been about traveller children finding life difficult in school.

## Racist bullying is the only type of bullying that schools must record

There is a difference between racial discrimination and racism. Racial discrimination means being treated differently to someone else because of your race, perhaps by being told you cannot wear a turban if you are a Sikh, a yarmulka if you are a Jewish boy or hijaab if you are a Pakistani girl.

Racism means you are subjected to abuse and harassment because of your race, colour or beliefs.

Bullying UK receives many complaints about racist bullying. If you are being bullied in this way you must tell your parents and ask them to write to your head teacher about it. Keep a diary of who says and does what because that will help the school to see where the bullying is taking place.

The complaints we've had include a girl aged six being told by a classmate that she cannot take the school mouse home because he doesn't like people with brown faces, to more serious incidents involving teenage gangs and weapons, one of which meant a boy was too frightened to return to school.

These complaints have come from all parts of the UK and are not confined to any particular area. Your parents need to make a complaint to the police if the school doesn't sort out racial bullying.

⇨ The above information is reproduced with kind permission from BullyingUK. Visit their website www.bullying.co.uk for more information.

*© Family Lives*

# What is homophobic bullying?

***Information from EACH.***

Just like any form of bullying or harassment, homophobia can include verbal, physical and emotional abuse by an individual or group but it's directed specifically at someone who is lesbian or gay or thought to be by others. What makes it different from other forms of bullying or harassment is the personal motivation that drives it.

Most homophobic bullying takes place at a time when young people are unsure about their own developing identity – subjected as they are to the confusing messages our society sends out about what it means to be 'a man' or 'a woman' and the stereotype of what it means to be gay. Homophobia presents itself in young people as the fear of and the reaction to an issue about which they can have little understanding and to a person perceived as 'different'.

Homophobic harassment of adults is unwanted behaviour which is offensive, causing the man or woman affected to feel threatened, humiliated or patronised. Such behaviour can seriously interfere with a person's personal health, work performance and security, creating a threatening living or workplace environment.

Homophobic bullying or harassment can take many forms:

⇨ unwanted physical contact

⇨ threatened or actual physical abuse or attack

⇨ verbal abuse such as suggestive remarks, jokes or name calling

⇨ display or distribution of offensive material or graffiti

⇨ non-verbal abuse such as mimicry, offensive gestures or body language.

⇨ The above information is reproduced with kind permission from Educational Action Challenging Homophobia. Visit their website www.eachaction.org.uk for more information.

---

# The curse of homophobic bullying

***Information from Press Association.***

***By Wes Streeting***

Yesterday's *Evening Standard* carried a moving article from Dr Christian Jessen, about a school friend who hanged himself because of homophobic bullying. Sadly, we know from many news stories around the world that Dr Christian's story isn't unique: gay young people often find themselves excluded, abused and attacked, to the point that many of them take their own lives.

News stories, of course, only give part of the picture. The full scale of homophobic bullying in Britain is today laid bare in a report from Stonewall, *The School Report 2012*, based on a national survey of over 1,600 gay young people by the University of Cambridge. The findings make distressing reading:

a quarter of gay young people say they've attempted suicide and over half have self-harmed, including cutting or burning themselves. Alarmingly, more than half of gay young people say they're homophobically bullied, one in six saying they've been physically abused. And 6% have received death threats.

Schools should be safe places where pupils flourish and teachers help them to excel. All too often, though, gay pupils walk through their school gates sweating with fear. Three in five of them even say teachers who witness homophobic bullying never intervene. And the problem doesn't stop with direct bullying. Almost all gay young people have heard homophobic language ('that's so gay' or 'you're so gay'), but only 10% say teachers challenge it.

It's alarming that any teacher would treat homophobic language as 'banter', but sadly there are some people – including prominent broadcasters and journalists – who suggest it's harmless to use 'gay' to mean 'rubbish'. There is, of course, a very simple objection to that: no-one accepts casual racist language, so why should we accept casual homophobia? Would it be inoffensive for young people (or DJs) to start saying 'that's so Asian,' or 'you're so black' when they mean 'that's crap' or 'you're a moron'? Of course not.

We can treat weak arguments with the scant respect they deserve, but anyone who suggests we shouldn't worry about playground taunts is colluding with bullies and spreading misery. More than four in five gay pupils say homophobic language distresses them. In schools where such language is never challenged, the rate of homophobic bullying stands at 68% – compared with 37% in schools where homophobic language is always challenged.

The consequences for gay pupils of bullying are severe. Nearly half of gay young people who've been homophobically bullied have skipped school, and a third change their educational plans because of it. Added to the clear mental health risks, *The School Report* draws a very clear conclusion: any failure to deal with homophobic language or bullying puts young lives and futures at risk.

The good news is it's not difficult to deal with homophobic bullying in an effective way. Stonewall works with thousands of schools around Britain who make sure they provide safe learning environments for all pupils. Whether that's by making sure incidents are dealt with quickly, broadening the curriculum to include gay issues or inviting gay role models to talk to young people, the outcome is always the same – a better school for everyone. Over the five years since Stonewall's 2007 school report, homophobic bullying overall has fallen from 65% to 55%. Action works – but inaction has terrible consequences.

Dr Christian's story about his late friend isn't unique. But with better school leadership and continuing support from the Government to put an end to homophobia, we're hopeful those sad stories will eventually be a thing of the past.

*5 July 2012*

⇨ The above information is reprinted with kind permission from the Press Association. Visit their website www. pressassociation.com for further information.

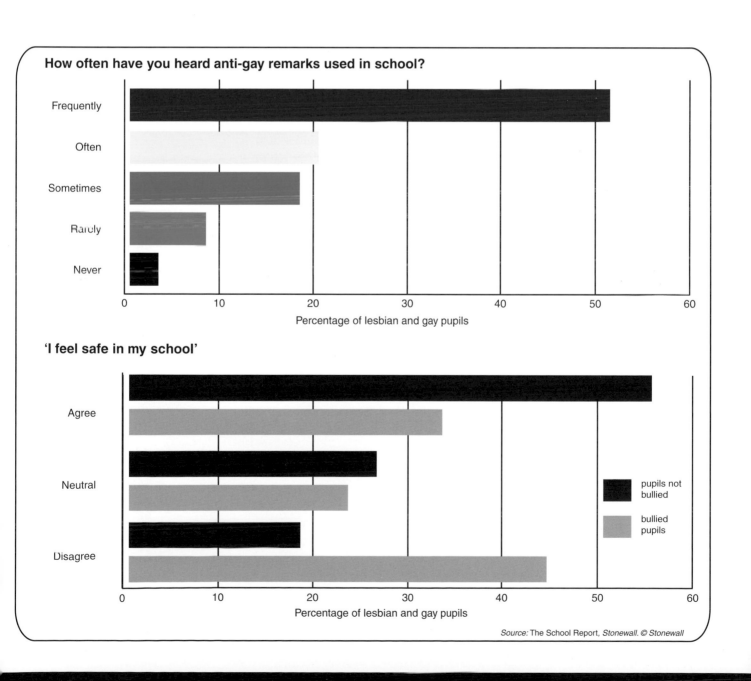

**How often have you heard anti-gay remarks used in school?**

Percentage of lesbian and gay pupils

**'I feel safe in my school'**

Percentage of lesbian and gay pupils

pupils not bullied

bullied pupils

*Source:* The School Report, *Stonewall.* © Stonewall

# Since when was racist bullying the only 'wrong' form of bullying?

## *Article from* **The Telegraph.**

### *By James Delingpole*

**W**hich is worse: bullying a child because they're (a) black, (b) pretty, (c) clever or (d) they have big blubbery lips?

Before you answer, have a look at Bullyonline – a website devoted to the dozens of children who have died, or nearly died, as a result of bullying by their peers. Here you will find 13-year-old Salvation Army girl Kelly Yeomans, who took a fatal overdose. There is Alistair Hunter, 12, who hanged himself after being spat on by bullies who used to urinate in his sports bag.

Perhaps some of the children on that heartbreaking list died as a result of racist abuse; or possibly, as a result of those nearly-but-not-quite-as-heinous modern crimes, 'homophobia' or 'disablism'. The majority, though, did not.

They were teased for the same reasons children have been teased since time immemorial: because they had a weakness which could be exploited.

In my case, my crime was to have big, blubbery lips. Never once did it occur to me that this might have been quite a sexy, Jaggeresque quality: all I could ever think of was how vile and ugly I looked and how dearly I wished that my lips were 'normal'.

Why did I wish this? Because the bullies who repeatedly called me 'Blubber Lips' spoke the phrase with such hatred, venom and disgust that I knew they must be right.

Did I suffer any more or less than a child bullied for the colour of their skin or for being a complete spaz at sports? I don't know. And here's the thing: nor do YOU know. Nor, in fact, does ANYONE know.

This is precisely what is wrong with treating 'racist' bullying as more heinous than any other form of bullying. It is based on a completely unprovable assumption which you can only make with confidence if you're either a self-hating (what other kind is there?) white liberal or a card-carrying member of the minority grievance industry.

Reading the case of the 15-year-old boy taken to court for repeatedly calling a female classmate 'wog', 'coon', 'gorilla' and 'golliwog', I don't think any of us could be in any doubt that the bully was a thoroughly nasty piece of work. I'm glad the poor girl has finally been freed of her tormentor. But I still don't understand what this case was doing in Lincoln magistrate's court – rather than being dealt with, as all such cases should, within the school system.

Or rather I do, all too well. It has to do with the dreaded 'r' word. If racism had not been involved, there is no way a 15-year-old boy would have faced criminal prosecution. The disgusting and morally purblind double standards here are wholly characteristic of New Labour and its politically correct decision to 'privilege' (as your typical Libtard would say) certain types of crime over others.

Kill someone because they're black or gay and you face a stiffer sentence than you would if you killed them, say, because you didn't like their poncy, upper-class accent.

New Labour would call this social justice.

Orwell called it Thought Crime.

*23 July 2009*

⇨ The above article originally appeared in *The Telegraph*. Visit their website www.blogs.telegraph.co.uk for more information.

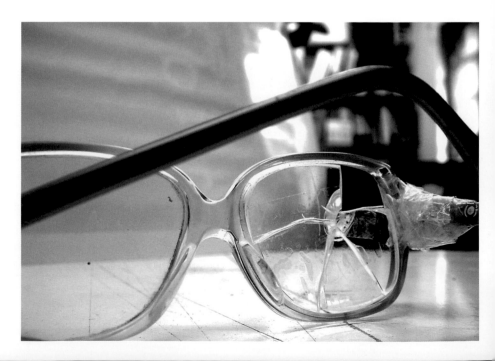

# Ten things you can do to challenge homophobia

*Information from EACH.*

## 1. Do not assume heterosexuality in general discussions about people.

Be inclusive in the language that you use, thereby avoiding marginalising lesbian, gay or bisexual young people and adults.

## 2. Make sure that homophobic bullying is identified in your organisation's bullying policy.

All equal opportunities policies should include a positive statement about sexuality, as they would about race, belief, disability, gender, etc.

## 3. Create a safe environment.

Use posters of Helpline numbers covering a range of issues to indicate that there is help available should people need it. Have nominated staff to whom young people and adults can turn included in this publicity.

## 4. Provide information.

Ensure appropriate books and information can be found in resource banks. Remove offensive books and materials.

## 5. Provide appropriate health information.

People identifying as gay or lesbian or unsure of their sexuality have an equal right to appropriate sexual health education as part of an organisation's Duty of Care.

## 6. Be a role model.

Actions speak louder than words. By adopting a consistently respectful behaviour to others' difference, ourselves, we can foster this in young people.

## 7. Be supportive.

If someone chooses you to discuss any issues about their sexuality it's because they respect you. Respect them for doing so and don't automatically refer them on to someone else/

## 8. Use your organisation's 'curriculum'.

Programmes of learning or education provide myriad opportunities to open up sensible, appropriate discussion around sexuality – take advantage of such 'teachable moments'. Don't regard issues of sexuality as the preserve of 'private life'.

## 9. Invite outside speakers to talk about difference, respect, understanding, prejudice, stereotpyes and discrimination.

Invite the local council's equality unit to assist by explaining how they address equality issues generally.

## 10. Request staff training as a matter of course.

Staff cannot be expected to understand how damaging homophobia is within their organisation's culture, and how important it is to support those affected by it, without professional guidance.

⇨ The above information is reprinted with kind permission from Educational Action Challenging Homophobia. Visit their website www.eachaction.org.uk for further information on this and other subjects.

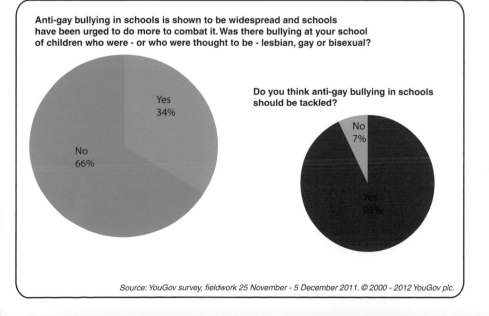

Anti-gay bullying in schools is shown to be widespread and schools have been urged to do more to combat it. Was there bullying at your school of children who were - or who were thought to be - lesbian, gay or bisexual?

Yes 34%

No 66%

Do you think anti-gay bullying in schools should be tackled?

No 7%

Source: YouGov survey, fieldwork 25 November - 5 December 2011. © 2000 - 2012 YouGov plc.

© EACH 2012 Ltd

# Have you been bullied for having red hair?

## Information from Everything for Redheads.

**M**orning all! I noticed a documentary project this morning, which made me remember my childhood, and experiences of being bullied for having red hair. Now I'm not going to whinge and moan, because there aren't many people out there who escape childhood without some teasing. Children can be cruel towards anything a bit different; there was a time when I would have given anything to have naturally blonde or brunette hair, but now I love my hair colour. It's a massive part of my identity for me, and I would be horrified at the idea of dying it.

Any teasing I received was minor, especially in comparison to some of the experiences mentioned in the video below, and some recent reports in the news about 'kick a ginger' day and teenagers being ambushed. I am still surprised to hear other people experiencing the same thing, and wondered what experiences some of you have had, or are still having?

### Ginger insults and names

While I'm not going to add fuel to the fire by providing bullies with names they haven't already come across, there are some names and insults we all know. Perhaps the reason that some people find the word 'ginger' distasteful when used to describe a hair colour is because it is hurled as an insult, and can be spat out with venom. The old favs;:Carrot Top, Copper knob, Duracell, Ginner, Ginger nut are quite tame, but there are certainly ones that make my lip curl. This is probably a personal thing, but for me Ginger Mhinger is pretty

offensive, tampon head is downright gross and Satan's love child...we've got red hair; we're not evil! Which names do you find most offensive? Including ones not mentioned?

### Being teased for red hair as an adult

Any comments I get now are laughable. For example, this year I have been shouted at across a petrol station forecourt, by grown men informing me that I am 'ginger'... which is lucky because I might not have remembered or noticed if they hadn't pointed it out. What considerate young men.

Passers by (again grown men) saying 'ginger minge' to me, is even more bewildering. But any comments now are mostly from men who have a slight 'thing' for redheads, which I'm never quite sure how to respond to ... are they even interested in me really or just my raven locks?

### The international spread of ginger bullying

While there was a time when being bullied for being ginger was mostly a British thing, it seems to have spread across the pond, aided by *South Park*. Statements that 'gingers have no souls' is going a bit far, but we're not the first group for *South Park* to pick on, we won't be the last, and it's not the worst thing they have said either. While I do find most of it amusing, the consequences of it aren't if it encourages bullying of red-haired classmates.

### Helping little redheads deal with teasing

While teasing and bullying can just

be a normal part of life, whatever age you are, being a bit different as a child does leave you more vulnerable to being picked on. This could be a particular challenge for parents who aren't redheads themselves, but have red-haired children. How do you help them? Well I'd say good role models to look up to is a good start; when you consider that a beautiful and talented artist such as Julianne Moore experienced teasing for having freckles it can certainly put things in perspective. To help, Julianne Moore has used her experiences of being teased for having freckles, to write a childrens book *Freckleface Strawberry* and the follow up *Freckleface Strawberry and the Dodgeball Bully*.

This charming book is a bright and humorous look at the way children deal with being different – from trying to hide their differences to finally embracing their unique characteristics – perfect for little redheads!

So what were your experiences growing up with red hair? How would you suggest to combat bullying? Do you have little red heads and are concerned about their experiences at school?

*11 October 2011*

⇨ The above information is reprinted with kind permission from Everything for Redheads. Visit their website www.everythingforredheads.co.uk for more information.

# Agony Aunt letters

## Tips to combat bullying.

### People make horrible comments because of my skin colour

Dear Agony Aunt,

The school I go to doesn't have many students who come from different backgrounds, so I kind of stand out because I am a different colour. People call me horrible names and tell me to go back to where I came from – the funny thing is is that I was born here and this is my home! Going to school is unbearable, how can I make these awful jokes and nasty comments stop?

– Abed

Hello Abed,

I am sorry to hear that you are having a hard time at school. These people are being ignorant with the nasty remarks they make about your colour, culture or background. This is racism and it is something serious that needs to be tackled.

Have a quiet word with your teacher to see if they can help you sort out the problem. If this doesn't work, get your parents to write a letter to the headteacher explaining what is happening. Your headteacher can then record the complaint and let your parents know how the situation is being dealt with (make sure to get it all in writing). Also, most towns now have Race Equality Councils who can help you and many police forces have officers who specially deal with schools. Not only can these organisations offer you help and understanding, but they can be very useful in warning off bullies.

We should celebrate our differences rather than single people out because of them.

– Agony Aunt

### I'm scared to answer my phone

Dear Agony Aunt,

There's this girl at school who has started to bully me. We used to be friends but now we don't get on anymore. I get nasty calls and text messages sent to my mobile phone. Sometimes when I answer I just hear heavy breathing down the phone and then the caller hangs up. I know that she's the one behind it because she says things from the text message that only the sender would know. I'm scared to answer my phone sometimes. Do you think the school will be able to do anything about it if my mum complains to them?

– Ashley

Hello Ashley,

When bullying occurs off school premises, they don't usually do anything about it. A few years ago, a High Court case said that schools didn't have to get involved, so sadly your school can't do anything to help here. However, in this case it is probably best to turn to the police.

Keep any threatening or offensive text messages, but do not reply to them. This may actually be considered an offence under the Telecommunications Act and could be classed as harassment.

If it is a particularly serious case, the police can check your phone and contact your mobile phone firm to find out where the messages are being sent from.

Another solution would be to change you mobile phone SIM card – lots of service providers offer free SIM card deals.

– Agony Aunt

### Don't want to tell parents or teacher and make matters worse

Dear Agony Aunt,

If my bag isn't being stolen, then I'm being called horrible names and pushed about. This one girl in particular starts it by saying mean things about me and then gets her friends to join in. I've seen her bully other people too, but I still feel so alone. I don't want to tell my parents or teachers because that will just make it worse. What should I do?

– Tess

Hello Tess,

Firstly, you must remember that the bullying is in no way your fault. If you really don't want to tell your parents or teachers, there may be ways you are able to protect yourself, or at least avoid the bullying. You said that you've noticed this girl bully other people too? I bet that other people in your class are wary of the girl bullying you (and maybe even them) and will sympathise with you. Try to make friends with these people, as they will understand what you are going through and you can help stand up to the bully together. Also, this means that you can avoid being alone, which is when bullies tend to strike.

However, if this continues, you must get help and support. Your school has a duty to keep you safe, and therefore safe from bullying. Pick a teacher you trust and have a quiet word with them about the problem. Plus, talking to your parents about it might not be so bad. Instead of them telling your teachers, they might be able to help you handle this situation better and offer their own self-help strategies. You could even ask them about their experiences with bullying.

– Agony Aunt

# What to do about bullying

*Whether you or someone you know is being bullied, make sure you tell someone who you trust what's going on. There's also a number of things you can do if you're bullying others and you want to stop it.*

## If you're being bullied

The first thing that you should do if you're being bullied is to tell someone about it. You shouldn't suffer in silence. You can tell a friend, a parent or a teacher at your school.

There are also a few things that you can do yourself that may make a person who bullies think twice about picking on you.

Try acting a bit more confidently – people who bully will often pick people out who seem quiet and reserved, so if you look like you're full of self-belief, it's likely they'll leave you alone.

If you get bullied on your way home from school, walk home with a group of friends or get an adult to collect you at the gate. It may sound embarrassing, but you'll be better protected if you're with a group of people.

Don't hit back. Although it's tempting, it's a bad idea as you may get yourself into trouble if you get involved in a fight.

## If you know or see someone being bullied

If you don't like seeing people being bullied, then do something about it. By not saying or doing anything, you're letting the person who bullies win and making the victim suffer for longer.

If you do want to do something, you can:

⇨ tell them to stop doing it, without getting yourself involved in a confrontation

⇨ let someone know about it like a teacher at your school or, if you see someone being physically attacked, you can report it to the police.

## If you're bullying others

It's often just as hard for people who have bullied others to ask for help. You may be worried that no-one will take you seriously or you'll get into trouble by admitting you've bullied someone. But that's not the case.

Try and talk to a teacher or an older pupil that you get on well with and talk through the reasons behind your bullying. They'll be able to give you support and advice about how to stop your bullying.

If you want to talk to someone anonymously, try calling Childline or the NSPCC. Although you may think that these organisations will only help victims, they're trained to help anyone in a confidential and non-judgemental way.

## Anti-bullying schemes at school

A lot of schools have an anti-bullying policy in place that aims to protect students against harassment and abuse. Try and get hold of a copy and bring it with you when you tell a teacher about the problems you're having.

Some schools also have older pupils who volunteer to be 'buddies' to victims of bullying. They can give you another way of reporting cases of bullying if you're not comfortable with talking to another adult.

If you know there's a bullying problem at your school, why not do something about it? There are a number of organisations that you can contact to help you set up an anti-bullying scheme or network. Even if you're not the person being bullied, you can still get involved.

## Useful contacts

⇨ Talk to FRANK

⇨ b-eat

⇨ NHS – Live WellOpens new window

⇨ Brook

⇨ The above information is reprinted with kind permission from Directgov. Visit their website www.direct.gov.uk for more information.

It's never as dark as it seems...

# Face bullying with confidence

## Eight skills kids can use right away.

*By Irene van der Zande, Kidpower Founder and Executive Director*

**M**ost harm caused by bullying is preventable! This article is from *Bullying – What Adults Need to Know and Do to Keep Kids Safe,* our bullying solutions book used by many families, schools and youth organisations to protect and empower their kids.

Unfortunately, bullying is a major problem in many schools and communities. Bullying prevention skills can protect kids from most bullying, increase their confidence, and help them to develop positive peer relationships. Here are some practices you can work on with the young people in your life now.

## 1. Walking with awareness, calm, respect and confidence

People are less likely to be picked on if they walk and sit with awareness, calm, respect and confidence. Projecting a positive, assertive attitude means keeping one's head up, back straight, walking briskly, looking around, having a peaceful face and body, and moving away from people who might cause trouble.

Show your child the difference between being passive, aggressive and assertive in body language, tone of voice and choice of words. Have your child walk across the floor, coaching him or her to be successful, by saying for example; 'That's great!', 'Now take bigger steps', 'Look around you' 'Straighten your back', etc.

## 2. Leaving in a powerful, positive way

The best self-defence tactic is called 'target denial', which means 'don't be there'. Act out a scenario where maybe your child is walking in the school corridor (or any other place where he or she might be bullied). You can pretend to be a bully standing by the wall saying mean things. Ask your child what these mean things might be because what is considered insulting or upsetting is different for different people, times and places.

Coach your child to veer around the bully in order to move out of reach. Remind your child to leave with awareness, calm and confidence, glancing back to see where the bully is. Let your child practise saying something neutral in a normal tone of voice like 'See you later!' or 'Have a nice day!' while calmly and confidently moving away. Point out that stepping out of line or changing seats is often the safest choice.

## 3. Setting a boundary

If a bully is following or threatening your child in a situation where she or he cannot just leave, your child needs to be able to set a clear boundary.

Pretend to poke your child in the back (do this very gently; the idea is not to be hurtful). Coach your child to turn, stand up tall, put his or her hands up in front of the body like a fence, palms out and open, and say 'Stop!'

Coach your child to have a calm but clear voice and use polite firm words – not whiney and not aggressive. Show how to do it and praise your child for trying – even though he or she does not get it right to begin with. Realise that this might be very hard and emotion triggering for your child (and maybe for you too).

Children need support to learn these skills. The idea is that your child takes charge of his or her space by moving away and, if need be, setting boundaries as soon as a problem is about to start – so that your child doesn't wait until the bullying is already happening.

## 4. Using your voice

If your child does get into a situation where somebody is trying to push or hit or knuckle his or her head, you could practise by holding your child gently and acting as if you are going to do the action gently. Coach your child to pull away and yell NO! really loudly. Coach him or her to say 'STOP! I don't like that!' Coach your child to look the bully in the eyes and speak in a firm voice with both hands up and in front like a fence. Teach your child to leave and go to an adult for help.

## 5. Protecting your feelings from name-calling

Schools, youth groups, and families should create harassment-free zones just as workplaces should. However, you can teach children how to protect themselves from insults. Tell your child that saying something mean back makes the problem bigger, not better.

One way to take the power out of hurting words by is saying them out loud and imagining throwing them away. Doing this physically and out loud at home will help a child to do this in his or her imagination at school.

Help your child practice throwing the mean things that other people are saying into a trash can. Have your child then say something positive out loud to himself or herself to take in. For example, if someone says, 'I don't like you', you can throw those words away and say, 'I like myself.' If someone says, 'You are stupid' you can throw those words away and say, 'I'm smart.' If someone says, 'I don't want to play with you' then you can throw those words away and say, 'I will find another friend.'

## 6. Speaking up for inclusion

Being left out is a major form of bullying. Exclusion should be clearly against the rules at school. A child can practise persisting in asking to join a game.

Pretend to be a bully who wants to exclude.

Have your child walk up and say, 'I want to play.' Coach your child to sound and look positive and friendly, not whiney or aggressive.

Ask your child the reasons that kids give for excluding him or her. Use those reasons so your child can practise persisting. For example, if the reason is, 'You're not good enough', your child can practise saying 'I'll get better if I practise!' If the reason is, 'There are too many already', your child might practise saying, 'There's always room for one

more.' If the reason is, 'You cheated last time', your child might practise saying, 'I did not understand the rules. Let's make sure we agree on the rules this time.'

## 7. Being persistent in getting help

Children who are being bullied need to be able to tell teachers, parents and other adults in charge what is happening in the moment clearly and calmly and persistently even if these adults are very distracted or rude – and even if asking for help has not worked before. Learning how to have polite firm words, body language and tone of voice even under pressure and to not give up when asking for help is a lifelong skill.

We have found that practise is helpful for both children and adults in learning how to persist and get help when you need it. Here is one you can do with your child.

Pretend to be a teacher or someone else who your child might expect help and support from. Tell your

child who you are pretending to be and where you might be at school. Have your child start saying in a clear, calm voice, 'Excuse me I have a safety problem.'

You pretend to be busy and just ignore your child! Coach him or her to keep going and say: 'Excuse me, I really need your help.'

Act irritated and impatient and say, 'Yes, what is it now?' and keep being busy.

Coach your child to say something specific like, 'The girls over there are calling me names and not letting me play with them. I have told them I don't like being called names and that I want to play but they won't listen.' or 'Those boys keep coming up and pushing me. I have tried to stay away from them but they keep coming up to me and won't leave me alone.' At school, teachers want children to try to solve their problems first. However, adult intervention is needed if this does not work.

You say: 'That's nice!' as if you heard but did not actually listen. This is very common for busy adults.

Coach your child to touch your arm and keep going 'Please, listen to me this is important.' Now you get irritated and say 'Can't you see I'm busy!?'

Tell your child that sometimes adults get angry and don't understand but not to give up in asking for help and to say the specific problem again: 'I do not feel safe here because (state specific problem again) _____.'

You minimise and say: 'What's the big deal? Just stay away from them.'

Coach your child to persistent and say again, 'Having this happen is making me feel bad about going to school. Please, I really need you to listen.'

Now change your demeanour so that your child can see you are listening and understanding and say 'Oh! I am sorry I yelled at you and I am glad you are telling me. Tell me more and we will figure out what to do.'

Remind your child that, if the adult still does not listen, it is not his or

her fault, but to keep asking until someone does something to fix the problem. Tell your child to please always tell you whenever he or she has a problem with anyone anywhere, anytime. Ultimately, it is the responsibility of adults to create safe environments for the children in their lives and to be good role-models for our children by acting as their advocates in powerful, respectful ways.

## 8. Using physical self-defence as a last resort

Children need to know when they have the right to hurt someone to stop that person from hurting them. At Kidpower, we teach that fighting is a last resort – when you are about to be harmed and you cannot leave or get help.

However, bullying problems are often not as clear-cut as other personal safety issues. Families have different rules about where they draw the line. Schools will often punish a child who fights back unless parents warn the school in writing ahead of time that, since the school has not protected their children, they will back their children up if they have to fight.

Learning physical self-defence helps most children become more confident, even if they never have to use these skills in a real-life situation. Just being more confident helps children to avoid being chosen as a victim most of the time. There are different self-defence techniques for bullying than for more dangerous situations – let your child practise a self-defence move like kicking someone in the shins, pinching someone's leg or upper arm or hitting someone in the chest. You can practise in the air or by holding a sofa cushion. Consider sending your child to a class like Kidpower.

Learn more about protecting kids from bullying in *Bullying: What Adults Need to Know and Do to Keep Kids Safe* and check out our comprehensive curriculum and guidebook for preventing abuse, kidnapping, bullying and other violence in our new book: *The Kidpower Book for Caring Adults: Personal Safety, Self-Protection, Confidence, and Advocacy for Young People.*

⇨ The above information is reprinted with kind permission from Kidpower. Visit their website www.kidpower.org for further information on this and other subjects.

*© 2011 Kidpower Teenpower Fullpower International*

---

# If you are a bully...

**Information from BullyingUK.**

Around 16 pupils in the UK kill themselves every year due to distress over bullying.

Their schools often say they had no idea what was going on. But the bullies know exactly what they've been doing – and so do their friends. It's too late to have regrets when someone has died, or been made so ill they need medical treatment.

## Bullying can make people feel really upset and depressed

Here is what some pupils told us in just one week:

'She has taken all my friends away and I go home at night and I'm depressed and cry' – girl aged 13

'One time I wouldn't eat because of people calling me "fat"' – boy aged 14

'Mondays were worst because I had to face the bully again and I soon got so worried it made me ill' – teenage girl

'I feel lonely and I want some advice about how to feel better about myself, going to school' – girl aged 15

'I feel like killing myself, it's that bad. I will probably end up in hospital, I have no friends and if I don't get help now I will end up a mess' – girl aged 14

'Other kids trip me up and call me names. It got so bad once that I ran away from school' – boy aged 12

'They stir things up so people don't want to be my friend. I'm depressed, annoyed, stressed and keep breaking down in tears. I feel like I'm about to fall apart' – boy aged 13

'I pray to make the bullies better people but it really upsets me because none of my friends stick up for me. They just sit there and laugh' – teenage girl

## You're a bully if you do any of these things to someone else:

⇨ You call them names

⇨ You make up stories to get them into trouble

⇨ You tell other people not to be friends with them

⇨ You make remarks about their culture, religion or colour

⇨ You make remarks about their disability or medical condition

⇨ You leave them out when you're choosing a games team

- You take away their possessions or demand money from them
- You hide their books or bag
- You send them nasty text messages or make silent calls to their phone
- You make threats about nasty things that will happen to them
- You make remarks about them liking other boys or other girls. This is called homophobic bullying
- You spread rumours about them
- You take their friends away leaving them on their own
- You hit them, kick them, trip them up or push them around
- You make remarks about their looks or weight
- You don't choose them to be your partner in class
- You tell them you're busy and then go off to enjoy yourself with other people
- You damage their property

- You make jokes about them when you can see they're upset
- You indulge in horseplay when you know they are not enjoying it
- You're going along with the crowd who are doing any of these things

## Risks you run if you bully someone else

You run quite a few risks if you bully someone else. You could get a warning, detention, temporary or permanent exclusion (expulsion). A violent, one-off incident harming another pupil could be grounds for expulsion.

If an incident involves violence, text phone, Internet abuse or demands for money then the victim and their parents should, and probably will, make a complaint to the police.

If you are over the age of criminal responsibility, which is ten in England and Wales, you could be charged with assault or harassment. Even if the case doesn't go to court

but results in a caution that could still have a serious effect on your future.

If you bully someone out of school the council or police could apply for an anti-social behaviour order (ASBO).

Bullies think that if they use false names on the Internet they can get away with it but they can't.

Some young people have been so upset they've killed themselves. There have been many cases where teenagers have killed themselves due to bullying and no doubt the bullies never thought this would be the consequence.

Bullying UK gets hundreds of emails a month and a surprising proportion are from secondary school pupils who say they are suicidal now or have been in the past. Some have been cutting themselves due to their distress. Others are receiving psychiatric and psychological help. Many of them are too frightened to go to school and some have been removed from school by their parents.

We also get emails from pupils suffering from eating disorders because they have been called fat when they are perfectly normal, and others from pupils with Aspergers syndrome who are teased because their condition makes it difficult to relate to other people.

Bullies also target those who are more clever, more popular and better looking than they are as well as those who stand out in any way perhaps because they wear spectacles, have red hair, dyslexia, diabetes or are just quiet and pleasant.

If you're bullying someone else do you really want to be responsible for another person having a mental breakdown and suffering unhappiness that can last a lifetime?

- The above information is reprinted with kind permission from BullyingUK. Visit their website www.bullying.co.uk for more information.

© Family Lives

# Britons are the world's most bullied workers, study reveals

**_Britons are among the world's most bullied workers, with seven in ten admitting to being bullied by bosses or colleagues._**

_By Kyrsty Hazell_

A survey by recruitment company Monster, questioning 16,517 workers in 53 countries, discovered a quarter of Brits find the bullying and cruel jibes so upsetting it dramatically affects their performance at work.

Some 10% admitted they had even been physically attacked in the workplace.

## 'Employers are responsible for a worker's health, safety and welfare while at work and should provide an atmosphere where people can get on with their job'

The research also found that our European counterparts also suffer badly from workplace bullying, with a staggering 83% claiming to be victims of physical or emotional bullying at work at some point in their career.

This compares to 65% of bullied Americans and 55% of harassed Asian workers. The survey also discovered that Spanish workers are most likely to be physically attacked while sensitive Dutch workers are the most likely to shed a tear due to work bullying.

Belgium had the lowest rate of workplace bullying, with 38%.

'Employers are responsible for a worker's health, safety and welfare while at work and should provide an atmosphere where people can get on with their job,' says Alan Townsend, Chief Operating Officer, Monster UK and Ireland.

'All companies should ensure they have clear policies and procedures for employees that are followed through by management. This can then prevent potentially dangerous outcomes such as poor workplace morale, lost productivity, litigation and health costs.'

These findings follow a previous study by Staffordshire University Business School which discovered that nearly 14 million British employees in the UK suffer from work bullying, according to BullyOnline.org.

With bullying now being commonplace in the British workplace, what should someone do if they experience this kind of adult bullying?

'If you are feeling bullied, confide in a manager or the Human Resources department in your workplace,' a spokesperson from Bullying UK told _The Huffington Post._

'This might not be so easy to do if it is a small organisation or you are being harassed or bullied by a manager. You could ask if they have a policy in place to deal with bullying and harassment at work. If you are a member of a trade union, you could get in touch with them and ask them for advice and representation. If you have house insurance, then you may be covered for legal expenses too, it's worth checking this.

'If you are looking to take this issue to an employment tribunal, you do need the best advice possible. Therefore, please get in touch with the Tribunals Helpline on 0845 959 775 so you are able to get advice on the steps you have to take.'

To identify whether you're being bullied at work, Directgov has compiled a list of examples of bullying behaviour:

⇨ Constantly picked on

⇨ Humiliated in front of colleagues

⇨ Regularly unfairly treated

⇨ Physically or verbally abused

⇨ Blamed for problems caused by others

⇨ Always given too much to do, so that you regularly fail in your work

⇨ Regularly threatened with the sack

⇨ Unfairly passed over for promotion or denied training opportunities.

If you're a victim of bullying in the workplace, find out how you should handle it with top tips from BullyOnline.org

_9 January 2012_

⇨ The above information is from _The Huffington Post_ and is reprinted with permission from AOL (UK) Limited. Visit their website www.huffingtonpost.co.uk for further information.

© 2012 AOL (UK) Limited

# Root causes of bullying behaviour in the workplace

**Information from Chartered Management Institute.**

*By Rebecca Kearley*

The Government's own estimates put the cost of bullying to the UK economy in the billions so recent accusations about bullying at No 10 must have hit a raw nerve. Research by CMI published at the end of 2008 put bullying behaviour in the workplace down to poor management.

It found that incidents of bullying were not just 'top down', with 63% of respondents observing bullying between peers and 30% witnessing subordinates bullying their manager.

The root causes of bullying were identified as:

⇨ Lack of management skills   70%

⇨ Personality clashes 57%

⇨ Authoritarian management styles 48%

⇨ Failure to address previous bullying 38%

⇨ Personal prejudice/discrimination 30%

⇨ Unrealistic targets and deadlines 23%

⇨ Inappropriate performance management systems 19%

⇨ Organisational change 10%

⇨ Demanding customers/clients 9%.

The research report, *Bullying at work: the experience of managers*, is free to download from www.managers.org.uk/bullying2008

CMI's professional practice guidance for managers on dealing with bullying in the workplace is free to download from www.managers.org.uk/bullyingguide

*25 February 2010*

⇨ Information from the Chartered Management Institute. Visit www.managers.org.uk.

*© Chartered Management Institute 2012*

---

# Bullying in the workplace

**Frequently asked questions from ACAS.**

What can I do about being bullied or harassed?

If you are being bullied or harassed, you should take any action you decide upon as quickly as possible. It is always best to try to resolve this informally in the first instance as sometimes a quick word can be all it takes. However, if this fails there are a number of options to consider:

⇨ see someone who you feel comfortable with to discuss the problem, perhaps someone in HR or a company counsellor

⇨ talk to your trade union or staff representative

⇨ keep a diary of all incidents, record: dates, times, witnesses, etc.

⇨ keep any relevant letter, emails, notes, etc.

Why should I as an employer act against bullying or harassment?

Bullying and harassment create an unhappy and unproductive workplace where you may have:

⇨ poor morale and poor employee relations

⇨ loss of respect for managers or supervisors

⇨ poor performance/lost productivity

⇨ absence/resignations

⇨ tribunal and other court cases and payment of unlimited compensation.

Through the Acas Helpline (08457 47 47 47) you can get advice on specific problems and explore alternatives to an Employment Tribunal claim, such as mediation or Pre-Claim Conciliation, where appropriate.

What can I do to prevent bullying or harassment taking place in my organisation?

There are a number of key considerations that should help to prevent this behaviour:

⇨ develop and implement a formal policy: this can be kept simple, but you should consider involving staff when writing it

⇨ set a good example: the behaviour of employers and senior managers is as important as any formal policy

⇨ maintain fair procedures for dealing promptly with complaints from employees

⇨ set standards of behaviour with an organisational statement about the standards of behaviour expected; this could be included in the staff handbook.

⇨ Information from ACAS. Visit their website www.acas.org.uk.

*© ACAS 2012, Euston Tower, 286 Euston Road, London NW1 3JJ*

# Chapter 2

# Cyberbullying – an introduction

*Cyberbullying is when one person or a group of people try to threaten or embarrass someone else using a mobile phone or the Internet. Cyberbullying is just as harmful as bullying in the real world. If you see it happening, report it. Don't ignore it.*

## Are you a part of it?

Those who take part in online bullying often use a group of friends to target their victims. They can ask others to add a comment to a photo on a blog, or forward something embarrassing onto another group of friends. Sometimes, these people don't even realise they're actually bullying someone.

## What forms can it take?

There are lots of different types of cyberbullying. These are the main ones:

### Email

Sending emails that can be threatening or upsetting. Emails can be sent directly to a single target, or to a group of people to encourage them to become part of the bullying. These messages or 'hate mails' can include examples of racism, sexism and other types of prejudice.

If someone sends you a message and you forward or laugh at it, you're actually adding to the problem.

### Instant messenger and chatrooms

Sending instant messenger and chatroom messages to friends or direct to a victim. Others can be invited into the bullying conversation, who then become part of it by laughing.

### Social networking sites

Setting up profiles on social networking sites to make fun of someone. By visiting these pages or contributing to them, you become part of the problem and add to the feelings of unhappiness felt by the victim.

### Mobile phone

Sending humiliating and abusive text or video messages, as well as photo messages and phone calls over a mobile phone. This includes anonymous text messages over short distances using Bluetooth technology and sharing videos of physical attacks on individuals (happy slapping).

### Interactive gaming

Games consoles allow players to chat online with anyone they find themselves matched with in a multi-player game. Sometimes cyber bullies abuse other players and use threats.

They can also lock victims out of games, spread false rumours about someone or hack into someone's account.

### Sending viruses

Some people send viruses or hacking programs to another person that can destroy their computers or delete personal information from their hard drive.

### Abusing personal information

Many victims of cyberbullying have complained that they have seen personal photos, emails or blog postings posted where others could see them without their permission.

Social networking sites make it a lot easier for web users to get hold of personal information and photos of people. They can also get hold of someone else's messaging accounts and chat to people pretending to be the victim.

## The effects of cyberbullying

Even though cyberbullying cannot physically hurt you, it can still leave you feeling mentally vulnerable and very upset. You can also feel scared, lonely and stressed and that there's no way out.

Escaping cyberbullying can be very difficult. Because anyone can get access to a mobile phone or the Internet almost anywhere, it can be tough for those on the receiving end to avoid it, even in the safety of their own home.

## Why do cyberbullies do it?

There's no simple answer for why some people choose to cause pain to others by bullying them. There are lots of possible reasons, but here are some common ones:

⇨ it can be simply a case of someone being in the wrong place at the wrong time and allowing themselves to be easily intimidated

- some people who cyberbully think that they won't get caught if they do it on a mobile phone or on the Internet
- the people who cyberbully are jealous, angry or want to have revenge on someone, often for no reason at all
- cyberbullies often think that getting their group of friends to laugh at someone makes them look cool or more popular
- some people also bully others as a form of entertainment or because they are bored and have too much time on their hands
- many do it for laughs or just to get a reaction.
- The above information is reprinted with kind permission from Directgov. Please visit their website www.direct.gov.uk for further information

# Cyberbullying

***Cyberbullying uses technology to harass, embarrass or threaten to hurt someone.***

Surveys have shown that around 50% of young teenagers have been bullied this way! The victims may feel unsafe, threatened, become depressed, withdraw from others and even seek to harm themselves.

Young people do often tease friends and kid around, but cyberbullying is not fun; it is something friends should not do to each other and there can be very serious effects, including suicide of the victim.

## If you're a victim

You might feel:

- guilty like it is your fault
- unsafe and afraid
- hopeless and stuck like you can't get out of the situation
- alone, like there is no one to help you
- depressed and feeling rejected by your friends and others
- confused and stressed out wondering what to do and why this is happening to you
- ashamed that this is happening to you.

## What to do

It is important that you tell and keep on telling until something is done about it. Bullies rely on their victims not speaking up so don't give them that satisfaction.

- Tell your parents or caregivers.
- Tell a teacher or counsellor at school if you suspect it is someone there. Every school has ways that they should follow for dealing with bullying, including cyberbullying.
- As with other types of bullying it is a good idea not to show that you are upset by firing back in the same way. Don't become a cyberbully yourself.

Remember, it is not your fault. There is nothing wrong with you. The behaviour of bullies is not OK. It is their responsibility.

- Tell yourself positive things about yourself every day, several times a day.
- Talk about it with friends who would be able to support you through a difficult time.
- Concentrate on positive things in your life.
- Do things that make you feel good.
- Build regular fun activities into your life.
- Do things that you know you're good at.
- Find new interests (they don't have to be expensive).
- Look at our topics about harassment that may help you.

If you know someone who is being cyberbullied then help them to get help. No-one should be made to feel threatened in this cowardly way.

The website 'Bullying no way' has lots of information on it that could be helpful http://www.bullyingnoway.com.au/

## So how can you keep yourself safe?

### Internet

If you want to join a social network like Facebook:

- Put everything behind password protected walls where only people you invite can see.
- Never give your password to anyone!
- Only allow people who are your real friends onto your friends list.
- Morph or blur any photos of yourself so that cyberbullies or would-be predators can't use them or parts of them to embarrass you.
- Don't post anything which could be used to embarrass you or that you wouldn't like someone you really respect to see.
- Don't do anything or say anything online that you wouldn't normally do or say offline.
- Protect your friends' privacy by not posting anything about

them without their permission. Insist on them protecting your privacy too.

⇨ Check your friends' comments and pics to make sure they are protecting your privacy and not opening you up to cyberbullying. They may not be as careful as you about protecting their safety and this could put you all at risk of predators.

⇨ Be aware that predators disguise themselves. The cool young friend you have made online could be a very different person from what you think!

### Email

Email is a great way to keep in touch with friends but remember that sharing emails around a group can lead to problems.

⇨ Don't give out your email address to people you don't know.

⇨ Ask friends to delete your name if they want to pass your message to someone else in their group.

⇨ Change your password often to protect yourself and your contact list.

⇨ Don't forward emails without deleting the name of the person who sent it to you. You can cut and paste the info to a new page if you can't delete the address of the person who sent it to you.

⇨ Don't forward messages without the sender's permission.

⇨ If you want to send a message to many people you can use the 'Bcc' field to ensure that the only address the receiver sees is their own.

⇨ Most security warnings about viruses are just hoaxes. But don't pass any on to others as you may be passing on problems for them and yourself.

⇨ If you don't know the sender of an email, then don't open it!

⇨ You can block emails by clicking on 'actions' then 'junk mail' and

choosing the 'add sender to blocked senders list' option.

### Mobile phones

Mobile phones are becoming so amazing that you can do just about anything you need to on a phone. Unfortunately cyberbullies have found them a great way to hurt or embarrass others.

So what can you do?

⇨ Don't give out your number to people you don't know. Ask friends never to pass on your number without checking with you first.

⇨ Don't leave your phone around so that others could see your number.

⇨ Maybe use caller ID blocking if you are making a call to someone you are not sure of.

⇨ If you are bullied in this way then don't respond to their call. Bullies like to see what effect they are having and may stop if they're not getting their kicks.

⇨ Keep any insulting or threatening SMS by saving them on your phone with the time and date, then show them to a trusted adult. If messages continue then go to the Police. They can find out the identity of the bully and will take action. It is against the law to use a mobile phone to harass or threaten someone.

⇨ If an unknown number comes up on your phone then answer without using your name in case it is a 'would-be bully' checking out they've got the right person. If it's a friend who has changed their number from the one on your contact list then you'll recognise their voice anyway.

⇨ Use your number only on your voicemail for the same reason.

⇨ If bullying continues turn off your phone and report it to your network provider. They will probably say change your number. This may be a good idea. It gives you the chance to check all your contacts and start again with a list of close friends and family.

## Things you should think about if you are a cyberbully

Have a look at this website (http://www.bullyingnoway.com.au) and read some of the stories about cyberbullying then ask yourself some questions.

⇨ Why am I behaving like this?

⇨ Is this respecting others or showing respect for myself?

⇨ What would I feel like if someone were doing this to me or my friend?

⇨ Is this the way to sort out problems?

⇨ What if everyone behaved like this, what would happen?

⇨ How will I feel if everyone finds out I have been bullying people in this way?

Then stop being a bully!

⇨ The above information is reprinted with kind permission from Women's and Children's Health Network. Visit their website www.wchn.sa.gov.au for more information.

*© Government of South Australia*

# Bullying on social networks

*Bullying isn't something that just happens in the real world. More and more teenagers are being bullied online through social networking sites. If you are getting threatening messages online, there are a number of ways to get them stopped.*

## What are online social networks?

There are lots of online social networks that let you chat with other Internet users.

You create your own profile and user name and fill in a few details about your likes and dislikes. Once you've done that, you can add music, videos and photos to your profile that other people can comment on.

You can also leave messages and comments on your friends' profiles.

They're great when you want to chat, share photos and play games with your friends and other people interested in the same things as you.

Social networks you may have heard of include:

- ⇨ MySpace
- ⇨ Facebook
- ⇨ Twitter
- ⇨ Bebo
- ⇨ Last.fm
- ⇨ FriendFeed
- ⇨ YouTube
- ⇨ Flickr.

## Bullying on social networks

Sadly, some people use social networks to tease and bully others.

Cyberbullies can:

- ⇨ post abusive messages on your profile wall
- ⇨ add rude comments to a picture you've uploaded
- ⇨ put a video or photo on their own profile that makes fun of someone and encourage their friends to send it to others.

Bullying on social networks can be tough to deal with, especially if a victim is being bullied by the same person at school.

Because it often happens on your own computer at home, online bullying can be very difficult to get away from.

If you feel like you're being bullied on your personal profile, there are some things you can do.

## Online friends

If you're getting bullied by a linked friend, block them or delete them from your list.

You may have fallen out with someone, but think you may become friends again in the future.

If this is the case, blocking them for a short time means you won't see any comments they may make that might upset you. You can always unblock the same person later.

If you're getting bullied by someone and they try to become your friend online, you can refuse their friend request. After all, why would you want to chat online with someone you don't get on with in the real world?

## Online privacy settings

Remember that most social networks let you control who can see different parts of your profile.

For example, you might only want to let members of your family and your closest friends see your photo albums.

You can even make your whole profile private. Doing this means no-one will be able to find it even if they look for your name in a search engine.

To find out how to control your privacy settings, have a look around your profile homepage for a link to 'safety tips' or 'privacy'.

## Fake online profiles

You may see a profile that has been set up by someone pretending to be you.

Fake profiles can be really upsetting, as they can be used to send abuse to others who may believe that it's actually you.

If you see a fake profile, report it to the social network's customer services department as soon as possible and ask them to delete it.

Some networks also have a 'report profile' button, which you can use if the profile is fake or offensive.

## Other general social media tips

If someone is bullying you on your own social profile page, you should:

- ⇨ keep and save any bullying emails or images you have been sent
- ⇨ take a screenshot of any comments that are threatening, but then delete them so you don't have to read them again
- ⇨ make a note of the time and date that messages or images were sent, along with any details you have about the sender
- ⇨ try changing your online user ID or nickname
- ⇨ not reply to any bullying messages or get into any online arguments.

Don't forget that anything you post online can be seen by anyone. This includes your parents, your boss or your teachers.

Use your common sense and think before you publish anything on your profile.

- ⇨ The above information is reprinted with kind permission from Directgov. Visit their website www.direct.gov.uk for more information.

© Crown copyright

# Bullying on mobile phones

*Receiving a rude text message or a threatening call on your mobile phone from a bully isn't just upsetting. It can be a criminal offence. If you are being bullied on your mobile phone, don't reply and let someone know as soon as possible.*

## How can you get bullied on a mobile phone?

Cyberbullying isn't just something that takes place on the Internet. You can also be cyberbullied if you get abusive calls and text messages on your mobile phone.

These calls, text messages and voicemails can be really upsetting, and it is often hard to understand how the sender knows your mobile phone number.

## 'Cyberbullying isn't just something that takes place on the Internet.'

If you think you are being bullied on your mobile phone, the most important thing is not to respond or get into an argument. Bullies are usually cowards, so showing a reaction is just giving them what they're after.

At the same time, that doesn't mean you should ignore it and do nothing.

## Types of mobile bullying

There are many ways that you can get bullied through your mobile phone.

### Scary phone calls

Victims of mobile phone bullying can receive abusive phone calls from someone who uses threats of violence to scare them.

Some bullies choose to stay silent on the other end of the phone, which is confusing and worrying for the person who answers the call.

### Abusive text messages

People who bully sometimes send text messages that try to scare, upset or hurt someone on purpose. Getting a message like this can be frightening, especially if it is from someone you don't know.

### Offensive picture messages

You may also be worried about photos and images that you have been sent over your mobile phone.

These could be pictures of you that have been taken without your knowledge. They could also be pictures that show you in situations that you would rather keep private.

### Embarrassing or violent videos

Most mobile phones come with a video camera now, which means being filmed without knowing it can happen more often.

If you're being bullied over your mobile phone, you might:

⇨ get videos of yourself that you didn't know were being filmed

⇨ see embarrassing mobile phone videos of yourself posted on video sharing websites like YouTube.

You may also have heard of 'happy slapping', where victims are physically assaulted and a video of the attack is then posted on the Internet.

## How to stop mobile phone bullying

Even though it's a hassle, the best way to stop mobile phone bullying is to get another SIM card or change your mobile number.

Once you have a new phone number, only give it out to members of your family and close friends.

If you get a bullying text, save it in your inbox. You should also make a note of the time you received the message, and the sender's details. Do not delete the message from your inbox.

Even though you might want to, the police or your mobile phone company may need it if they investigate.

## Don't suffer in silence

If you are being targeted by mobile phone bullies, it's important to let someone know. If you feel uncomfortable talking to a parent or a teacher, try another older relative or friend who you trust. They will be able to help you stop the bullying.

You should also report the bullying to your mobile phone company. They may be able to trace the person who is calling or texting you, even if they withhold their number.

Mobile phone companies all deal with bullying differently, so contact the customer helpline to find out who to speak to.

If you would like more confidential advice, you can contact ChildLine.

## The police and mobile phone bullying

Making offensive calls is actually a criminal offence. Anyone who is found guilty could have to pay a large fine. They may also be given a six-month prison sentence.

If you are being bullied over your mobile phone, don't be afraid to report it to the police.

⇨ The above information is reprinted with kind permission from Directgov. Visit their website www.direct.gov.uk for more information.

*© Crown copyright*

# Cyberbullying affects one in five youngsters in UK

*As many as one in five young people could be affected by cyberbullying, according to research carried out by academics at Anglia Ruskin University.*

The study, commissioned by leading children's charity the National Children's Bureau on behalf of its Wellcome Trust-funded PEAR young people's group, examined the scale of cyberbullying and the negative effect it has on young people's mental health.

Cyberbullying is a relatively new problem which involves people using the Internet or mobile phones to distribute text or images to harass, hurt or embarrass another person.

Niamh O'Brien, Research Fellow, Steven Walker and Dr Tina Moules, Director of Research in the Faculty of Health, Social Care and Education at Anglia Ruskin University, led the research amongst young people aged ten to 19 and discovered that cyberbullying was far more prevalent amongst girls. Amongst the young people surveyed, 18.4% admitted to being a victim of cyberbullying and 69% of those bullied were girls.

More girls than boys had also witnessed cyberbullying, known somebody who had been cyberbullied or known somebody who had cyberbullied others.

Of those who said they had been affected by cyberbullying the most common effects were on their confidence, self-esteem and mental and emotional well-being. Over a quarter of those who had been cyberbullied (28.8%) said that they had stayed away from school and over a third (38.9%) had stopped socialising outside school as a result of cyberbullying.

Most young people thought cyberbullying was just as harmful as other forms of bullying (74.4%). Some thought it was far worse because this bullying is permanent in written or picture format, could get very personal and be transmitted to many more people more quickly.

It was also suggested that the secretive nature of cyberbullying caused additional fear in the victim. Also, because cyberbullying can take place at any time and in any place, options for escape are limited.

Of those who had sought support to deal with cyberbullying, most said that they had spoken to their parents/carers, while nearly half had approached a teacher or someone else in school. Reasons for not seeking support included a fear of making the cyberbullying worse and feeling that they were able to deal with the incident themselves.

Some key strategies used by young people to deal with cyberbullying included: changing or blocking their instant messenger, email addresses and mobile numbers; and being careful who they gave their personal details to. Only a small minority took action by reducing their use of social networking sites.

*2 August 2011*

⇨ The above information is reprinted with kind permission from Anglia Ruskin University. Visit their website www.anglia.ac.uk for more information.

*© 2012 Anglia Ruskin University*

# EU Kids Online – bullying summary

**Research highlights for Children's Online Safety.**

## Aims

The EU Kids Online Project aims to enhance knowledge of European children's and parents' experiences and practices regarding use of the Internet and new online technologies, informing the promotion of a safer online environment for children.

## Key findings

### Main messages

⇨ 93% of nine to 16-year-old Internet users in Europe have neither bullied nor been bullied online. Those who have bullied or been bullied online are more vulnerable psychologically or from their socio-demographic background.

⇨ Bullying, and having been bullied online mostly go hand in hand. Around 60% of those who bully have been bullied by others. Bullying and being bullied by others mostly occur through similar modes. Of those who have bullied others offline, 57% have been bullied, though only 10% were bullied online. Of those who have bullied others online, a similar number have been bullied (58%) but 40% online.

### Prevalence

⇨ Across Europe, 6% of nine to 16-year-olds who use the Internet report having been bullied online while only half as many (3%) confess to have done so.

⇨ Girls, younger children and those from a low socio-demographic background report more often being victims of bullying and less often to bully others than boys, older children and those with a higher socio-demographic background.

⇨ Of those who say that they have bullied others online (3%), one third (1%) also say that they themselves have been bullied online and among those 5% who state that they have been bullied online, one in five admits to also having bullied others online – bullying and being bullied online are not two distinctive phenomena but go hand in hand.

⇨ There are three bullying groups – (i) those who bully, (ii) those who have been bullied and (iii) those who have both experienced bullying and bullied others.

### Bullying and vulnerability

Two measures of psychological vulnerability were applied to respondents.

⇨ Sensation seeking

  ⇨ The two bullying groups show higher sensation seeking compared to those neither having bullied nor having been bullied online.

⇨ Those who have bullied or are bullies and victims are higher in sensation seeking than those who are bully victims but not bullies.

⇨ Ostracism

  ⇨ Those who have been bullies, bully victims or both (bullies and victims) show higher ostracism than those who experienced neither. Further, bully victims show higher ostracism than bullies.

Taken together, these findings suggest that psychological difficulties are associated with both online bullying and victimisation, sensation seeking with online bullying, and ostracism with victimisation from online bullying. Moreover, those involved in online bullying show overall a higher psychological vulnerability than those not involved in online bullying.

### Responses to bullying

⇨ Around 40% of those who have not bullied say they 'tried to fix the problem' while this response was given by about 10% less (~30%) among both the offline and online bullies.

⇨ Less than 10% of those who have not bullied 'felt a bit guilty about what went wrong'. However, this response increased by at least half (+5%) among offline and online bullies.

THE BULLIED ..... BECOMES THE BULLY

⇨ One in three who had bullied others online said that they try to get back at the other person when being bullied online.

## Policy context

Policies for the promotion of a safer Internet are based on an understanding of risks and risk-taking behaviour. The EU Kids Online Project provides a vast array of quantitative data relating to the online behaviour of children and young people in the UK. An understanding of broad trends in patterns of risky use of the Internet and new online technologies is essential for the development of evidence-based policies for the promotion of safer Internet use.

## Methodology

In this large-scale quantitative study, the survey was administered face-to-face at home to a random stratified sample of 25,142 children aged nine to 16 who use the Internet, plus one of their parents, during Spring/Summer 2010 in 25 European countries.

## Background

The UK survey was conducted as part of a larger 25 country survey conducted by the EU Kids Online network and funded by the EC's Safer Internet Programme.

Source: www.eukidsonline.net

Research Team Sonia Livingstone, Leslie Haddon, Anke Görzig and Kjartan Ólafsson

Contact information S.Livingstone@lse.ac.uk

October 2011

⇨ The above information is reprinted with kind permission from UKCCIS Evidence Group. Visit their website www.saferInternet.org.uk for more information.

© UKCCIS Evidence Group

# The 12 types of Internet troller

*The 12 types of troller are quite unique. Some are quite similar and differing in that one group posts kudos to be friendly and the other flames to be nasty.*

*By Jonathan Bishop*

**Lurker –** Silent calls by accident, etc., clicking on adverts or 'like' buttons, using 'referrer spoofers', modifying opinion polls or user kudos scores.

**Elder –** An elder is an out bound member of the community, often engaging in 'trolling for newbies', where they wind up the newer members often without questioning from other members.

**Troll –** A Troll takes part in trolling to entertain others and bring some entertainment to an online community.

**Big Man –** A Big Man does trolling by posting something pleasing to others in order to support their world view.

**Ripper –** A Ripper takes part in self–deprecating trolling in order to build a false sense of empathy from others.

**Flirt –** A Flirt takes part in trolling to help others be sociable, including through light 'teasing'.

**Snert –** A Snert takes part in trolling to harm others for their own sick entertainment.

**MHBFY Jenny –** A MHBFY Jenny takes part in trolling to help people see the lighter side of life and to help others come to terms with their concerns.

**E–Venger –** An E–Venger does trolling in order to trip someone up so that their 'true colours' are revealed.

**Wizard –** A wizard does trolling through making up and sharing content that has humorous effect.

**Iconoclast –** An Iconoclast takes part in trolling to help others discover 'the truth', often by telling them things completely factual, but which may drive them into a state of consternation. They may post links to content that contradicts the worldview of their target.

**Chatroom Bob –** A Chatroom Bob takes part in trolling to gain the trust of others members in order to exploit them.

⇨ Information from The Crocels Trolling Academy. Visit their website www.trollingacademy.org for more information.

© The Crocels Trolling Academy

# What is trolling? And why do people do it?

***The word comes from a Norse monster but the troll is a very modern menace.***

Trolling is a phenomenon that has swept across websites in recent years. Online forums, Facebook pages and newspaper comment forms are bombarded with insults, provocations or threats. Supporters argue it's about humour, mischief and freedom of speech. But for many, the ferocity and personal nature of the abuse verges on hate speech.

In its most extreme form it is a criminal offence. Last year, Sean Duffy was jailed for 18 weeks after posting offensive messages and videos on tribute pages about young people who had died. One of those he targeted was 15-year-old Natasha MacBryde, who had been killed by a train. 'I fell asleep on the track lolz' was one of the messages he left on a Facebook page set up by her family. Colm Coss was jailed for 18 weeks after posting obscene messages on Facebook sites set up in memory of Jade Goody, the Big Brother star, and several other dead people.

Trolling appears to be part of an international phenomenon that includes cyberbullying. Cyberbullying is when one person or a group of people try to threaten, tease or embarrass someone else by using technology, such as a mobile phone or the Internet, and it is just as harmful as bullying in the real world. Trolling is a broad term, taking in everything from a cheeky provocation to violent threats.

A recent suspected victim of trolling and cyberbullying is model Claudia Boerner, who was found dead in her flat in Germany. While the circumstances surrounding her death aren't yet clear, it is widely believed to be connected to the staggering amount of online abuse she received after starring in the German version of TV's *Come Dine With Me*.

Why people troll continues to baffle the experts.

'Online people feel anonymous and disinhibited,' says Prof Mark Griffiths, director of the International Gaming Research Unit at Nottingham Trent University. 'They lower their emotional guard and in the heat of the moment may troll either reactively or proactively. It is usually carried out by young adult males for amusement, boredom and revenge,' he adds. 'And often they'll say something online that they'd never dare to say to your face.'

Perhaps trolls and cyberbullies don't realise the extent of the harm and suffering they can cause. Or perhaps they do, but they just don't care.

## What does the law say?

The Communications Act 2003 governs the Internet, email, mobile phone calls and text messaging.

Under section 127 of the act it is an offence to send messages that are 'grossly offensive or of an indecent, obscene or menacing character', and the offence occurs whether those targeted actually receive the message or not.

So a good reason to think twice if you're thinking of trolling!

## A few other things to consider...

Don't tweet, blog, message or post online anything that you wouldn't say directly to someone's face.

If you're posting a criticism of anyone or anything, be careful how you express it. Can you do it without resorting to a personal attack?

Remember that the Internet is public and every time you tweet, blog or post, you are publishing or broadcasting. Once you have posted something online, you can't take it back and the damage could be done within seconds.

Don't forget that there is a human being on the receiving end of every comment you make.

If you have been a victim of trolling or just want to find out more about how to stay safe on the Internet, check out our pages on Staying Safe and the ThinkuKnow site.

*23 April 2012*

⇨ The above information is reprinted with kind permission from Teen Wirral. Visit their website www.teenwirral.com for more information.

© 2010 Wirral Council

ANONYMITY

# Teachers report widespread cyberbullying by pupils and parents

*Two-fifths report they have been abused on social networking sites, while almost half of those felt unsupported by their school.*

*By Hélène Mulholland*

Teachers have been issued with death threats, accused of serious crimes including paedophilia and rape, and subjected to sexist and racist abuse, according to a poll revealing widespread cyberbullying by pupils – including some still at primary school – as well as parents.

The scale of bullying by pupils on social networking sites against those trying to educate them is suggested in an online survey due to be released on Saturday by the teaching union, the NASUWT, at its annual conference in Birmingham being held over the Easter bank holiday weekend.

While the majority (60%) of pupils involved were between 11 and 16, others were younger – with one reported incident involving a five-year-old. Parents were also using social networks to comment about them, according to 16% of teachers.

The report also highlights the lack of support felt by many teachers after they report incidents to their school.

Of those who took part in the survey, more than two-fifths (42%) said they had been a victim of cyberbullying. Of these, 61.2% said they had been subjected to a pupil writing an insulting comment about them on a social network or Internet site, 38.1% said a student had made comments about their competence or performance as a teacher, and 9.1% said they had faced allegations that they behaved inappropriately with pupils.

One member revealed that a student went on Facebook to say he would 'cut my f****ing throat when he saw me', yet no action was taken against the pupil.

An English teacher reported that a pupil posted on Facebook that they 'should actually die' and swore about them.

Another teacher reported that his partner's children were distressed after a pupil alleged on Facebook their relationship had begun while she was still with her husband. Again, no action was taken against the pupil.

Almost two-thirds (64%) reported the incidents, with almost half (46%) left feeling the sanction taken against the pupil was inadequate or that no action was taken at all. Only 32% felt the appropriate action was taken.

Almost half (49%) of teachers who were subjected to abusive comments from parents said they did not feel supported or had no action taken as a result, with just 29% feeling that appropriate action was taken.

The social network of choice for most pupils levelling abuse at their teachers was Facebook (77%), while 21% used RateMyTeachers. com, 6% used Twitter and 1% used MySpace.

Chris Keates, leader of the union, said some of the findings were 'truly shocking' and warned that unacceptable abuse would continue to rise unless the Government and employers took it seriously.

Keates said the survey findings exposed the way some employers were failing in their duty of care towards staff by not having appropriate policies in place nor taking incidents seriously when reported.

She added: 'But it is the Coalition government that is found most seriously wanting.

**'Of those who took part in the survey, more than two-fifths (42%) said they had been a victim of cyberbullying.'**

'Until this Coalition took office, there was comprehensive guidance in place nationally, providing details of teachers' legal rights and entitlements and a suite of good practice for schools to use to protect teachers and pupils from this kind of abuse.

'This has now been reduced to just one paragraph on cyberbullying, sacrificed on the altar of this Coalition's flawed and distorted so-called policy of reducing bureaucracy and demonstrating its lack of concern for the well-being of staff.

'Until the Government and teachers' employers recognise that the welfare of the workforce is important and these issues must be tackled seriously, this unacceptable abuse will not only continue but is likely to escalate.'

*7 April 2012*

⇨ The above article originally appeared in *The Guardian*. Visit their website www.guardian.co.uk for further information.

# Cyberbullying – supporting school staff

**Information from Association of Teachers and Lecturers (ATL).**

## What is cyberbullying?

Some features of cyberbullying are different to other forms of bullying:

⇨ Cyberbullying can take place 24/7. Incidents can take place in the victim's own home, intruding into spaces that have previously been regarded as safe and private.

⇨ The audience can be very large and reached rapidly. The difficulty in controlling electronically circulated messages means the scale and scope of cyberbullying can be greater than for other forms of bullying. Electronically forwarded content is hard to control and the worry of content resurfacing can make it difficult for the person being bullied to move on.

⇨ The profile of the person being bullied and bully may not rely on traditional power imbalances – a cyberbully may not be older, or physically stronger, or hold a position of greater authority than their victim.

⇨ Unlike other forms of bullying, the target of the bullying will have evidence of its occurrence. The bully will leave a 'digital footprint' that can potentially be used as evidence against them.

⇨ In some cases, incidents of cyberbullying may be unintentional. The person responsible may not realise that remarks are publicly accessible and persistent, or understand the amplified effect that technologies produce. They may not be fully aware of the potential seriousness or impact of their actions. Therefore prevention activities are key to ensuring the whole-school community clearly understands the serious consequences of cyberbullying, including sanctions.

## The scale of cyberbullying against school staff

Current research into the frequency of and impact on school employees of cyberbullying is not extensive. We do know that cyberbullying incidents can be extremely upsetting – even devastating – for the person being bullied, whatever age they are.

Cyberbullying of school staff is an issue that schools need to address within their whole-school cyberbullying strategy.

⇨ 15% of teachers responding to a 2009 survey carried out by Teacher Support Network and The Association of Teachers and Lecturers reported they had been victims of cyberbullying.

http://icanhaz.com/teachersupport

⇨ 46% of teachers surveyed for *Becta's E-Safety and Web 2.0* report (September 2008) reported negative experiences caused by pupils using web 2.0 technologies (defined as participatory mobile and web-based sites and services).

http://icanhaz.com/BECTAsurvey

⇨ In May 2007 the NASUWT surveyed teachers over a period of five days on cyberbullying. Almost 100 teachers reported incidents of cyberbullying by pupils using mobile phones and web-based sites that had caused real distress and trauma.

www.nasuwt.org.uk/cyberbullying

School workforce unions, professional associations and industry providers have noted an increase in cyberbullying reports and related inquiries, and are committed to working with the DCSF to reduce incidence and support schools to deal with incidents effectively. All forms of bullying, including cyberbullying, should be taken seriously. Bullying is never acceptable, and should never be tolerated.

## Cyberbullying and law

While there is not a specific criminal offence called cyberbullying, activities can be criminal offences under a range of different laws, including:

⇨ The Protection from Harassment Act 1997

⇨ The Malicious Communications Act 1988

⇨ Section 127 of the Communications Act 2003

⇨ The Public Order Act 1986

⇨ The Defamation Acts of 1952 and 1996.

Cyberbullying in the form of discrimination or harassment of a member of staff by another member of staff may result in a situation where the governing body of a school has breached its duties under discrimination legislation.

It is the duty of every employer to ensure, so far as reasonably

'Pupils set up a web page with photographs taken on a mobile phone in school, obviously without me knowing. The site included threatening comments and offensive language. I printed the pages of the site to keep a hard copy and this was used to investigate who was responsible. The Principal interviewed all the pupils involved with their parents and has excluded the main author of the site until her exams in May. Others had fixed-term exclusions ranging from two to five days depending on the severity of their comment.'

*A staff member*

# Social networking sites

Contacts of some social network providers:

## Bebo

Reports can be made by clicking on a 'Report Abuse' link located below the user's profile photo (top left-hand corner of screen) on every Bebo profile page. Bebo users can also report specific media content (i.e. photos, videos, widgets) to the Bebo customer services team by clicking on a 'Report Abuse' link located below the content they wish to report.

www.bebo.com/Safety.jsp

## Facebook

Reports can be made by clicking on the 'Report' link located on pages throughout the site, or by email to abuse@facebook.com.

www.facebook.com/safety

## MySpace

Reports can be made by clicking on the 'Contact MySpace' link at the bottom of every MySpace page and selecting the 'Report Abuse' option. Alternatively, click on the 'Report Abuse' link located at the bottom of each user profile page and other user-generated pages. Inappropriate images can be reported by clicking on the image and selecting the 'Report this Image' option. Additionally, school staff may email MySpace directly at schoolcare@myspace.com

www.myspace.com/safety

practicable, the health, safety and welfare at work of all employees.

Incidents that are related to employment, even those taking place outside of the hours or place of work, may fall under the responsibility of the employer.

## Images and video

Taking pictures and creating short films is easier than ever before. Employees and learners can use mobile phones, digital cameras, camcorders and webcams to capture, edit and share images. Photo and video-sharing websites are extremely popular, and can be used effectively for school projects and presentations. It's important that employees and pupils are clear about their rights and responsibilities regarding taking pictures and making films.

⇨ Photos taken for official school use may be covered by the Data Protection Act and pupils and parents should be advised why they are being taken. Schools should consider e-safety issues when using pictures of pupils.

⇨ Photos taken for personal use are exempt from the Data Protection Act.

It is important to seek permission before sharing or posting a picture of someone publicly online. If a picture causes distress, the subject should ask the poster to remove it in the first instance and if this does not result in the image being taken down, a request can be made to the service provider to remove the picture or film that was taken and/or posted without consent.

Consent and rights management are important topics to address with the whole-school community. The acceptable use of equipment for creating images and film (which may most typically be camera-equipped mobile phones) should be accounted for within the appropriate behaviour policy and agreements. Schools should clearly communicate expectations, acceptable conduct and potential sanctions regarding inappropriate image taking and use by staff, pupils and parents.

# Video and photo hosting sites

## YouTube

Logged-in YouTube members can report inappropriate content by using the 'flag content as inappropriate' function which appears under every video.

http://icanhaz.com/YouTubeAbuseSafety

## Flickr

Reports can be made via the 'Report Abuse' link which appears at the bottom of each page. Logged-in members can use the 'flag this photo' link to report individual pictures.

www.flickr.com/guidelines.gne

# Chatrooms, individual website owners/forums, message board hosts

It is good practice for chat providers to have a clear and prominent reporting mechanism to enable the user to contact the service provider. Users that abuse the service can have their account deleted. Some services may be moderated, and the moderators will warn users posting abusive comments or take down content that breaks their terms of use.

---

Both pupils and employees should take care not to attach any significant personal information to publicly posted information, for example full names, without informed and/or parental consent. Even with consent, care should be taken to be mindful of basic e-safety practice.

## Getting content taken down

Where online content is upsetting and inappropriate, and the person or people responsible for posting is known, the quickest way to get material taken down is likely to be to ensure that the person who posted it understands why the material is unacceptable and to request that they remove it.

If the person responsible has not been identified, or will not take material down, the school leadership team member will need to contact the host (for example, the social networking site) to make a report to get the content taken down. The material posted may breach the service provider's terms and conditions of use and can then be removed.

In cases where the victim's personal identity has been compromised – for example, where a site or an online identity alleging to belong to the victim is being used, the victim will need to establish their identity and lodge a complaint directly with the service provider. Some services will not accept complaints lodged by a third party. In cases of a mobile phone abuse, for example, where the person being bullied is receiving malicious calls or messages, the account holder will need to contact their provider directly. Before a school or individual contacts a service provider, it's important to be clear about where the content is – for example by taking a screen capture of the material that includes the URL or web address. If you are requesting they take down material that is not illegal, be clear how it contravenes the site's terms and conditions.

In cases of actual/suspected illegal content, the schools designated representative should contact the police. The police will be able to determine what content is needed for evidential purposes.

⇨ The above information is reprinted with kind permission from Association of Teachers and Lecturers (ATL). Visit their website www.atl.org.uk for more information.

© 2012 Association of Teachers and Lecturers

# Instant Messenger

It is good practice for Instant Messenger (IM) providers to have visible and easy-to-access reporting features on their service. Instant Messenger providers can investigate and shut down any accounts that have been misused and clearly break their terms of service. The best evidence for the service provider is archived or recorded conversations, and most IM providers allow the user to record all messages.

Contacts of some IM providers:

## MSN

When in Windows Live Messenger, clicking the 'Help' tab will bring up a range of options, including 'Report Abuse'.

## Yahoo!

When in Yahoo! Messenger, clicking the 'Help' tab will bring up a range of options, including 'Report Abuse'.

# Tweeter jailed for racist abuse

**A student has been jailed after posting racist messages about Bolton Wanderers player Fabrice Muamba.**

*By Ian Dunt*

Liam Stacey, 21, posted comments about the player after he collapsed on the pitch from a heart attack during an FA Cup game against Tottenham earlier this month.

Several users complained to police about the comments from the Swansea University student.

Stacey claimed the account had been hacked and also attempted to delete the page in an effort to distance himself from the ensuing row, the court heard.

A police interview saw the student claim he was drunk when he sent the tweets.

Speaking to the court, prosecuter Lisa Jones said: 'Fabrice Muamba collapsed on the pitch and was believed to have died. Shortly after, Stacey posted on Twitter: "LOL, F**k Muamba. He's dead".'

When other users criticied Stacey, he replied with further offensive and racist abuse, Ms Jones said.

He texted a friend to say: 'I said something about Muamba that I shouldn't have and tweeted back to some people who abused me. Getting police on me now, which isn't good at all.'

In the initial bail judgement, Stacy was banned from using Twitter and other social media sites.

He has now been jailed for 56 days.

The speed of the arrest and the severity of the sentence are signs police are intent on cracking down on racist and abusive posts on the social media site.

*27 March 2012*

⇨ The above information is reprinted with kind permission from Politics.co.uk. Visit their website www.politics.co.uk for further information.

# Cheryl Cole reveals Internet bullying hell: 'people say I look fat'

**Cheryl Cole is the latest star to come forward and speak out against online bullies.**

The singer has revealed she has been subjected to vicious attacks, on Twitter and Facebook, for more than a year.

Cole spoke about the cyber bullies as she told *Grazia* magazine that she could relate to the teenagers helped by her charity, The Cheryl Cole Foundation.

'I get what these kids have gone through because I had a tough upbringing and I understand what it feels like to get bullied like some of them,' she said of growing up while living on a tough Newcastle council estate.

The former *X Factor* judge added: 'In the last few years, I've been bullied on Facebook and Twitter. It's evil and very public.

'People judge my appearance and hair, and say that I look fat.'

Speaking while meeting some of the teenagers that her Foundation has worked with, she told the magazine: 'I want to help these young people because I know how it feels to come out on the other side and be someone who achieves.'

Last week, TV couple Eamonn Holmes and Ruth Langsford said they have been the targets of Internet trolls, while in March, former *Blue Peter* presenter Richard Bacon said that he has been subjected to online abuse.

The Cheryl Cole Foundation helps The Prince's Trust work with young people in the North East.

She said of the Prince of Wales: 'The first time I had tea with him at Clarence House, I had an etiquette lesson on how to address him.

'But I forgot to say Prince and just called him Charles, which was embarrassing and someone started coughing at my mistake behind me to correct me. But he couldn't stop laughing,' she said.

⇨ The above information is from *The Huffington Post* and is reprinted with permission from AOL (UK) Limited. Visit their website www.huffingtonpost. co.uk for further information.

# Responding to cyberbullying

## Top ten tips for teens

*By Sameer Hinduja, Ph.D. and Justin W. Patchin, Ph.D.*

### 1. Take a stand

When you see someone being bullied, step in and do something about it. Tell them to stop. If a cyberbully receives criticism from their peers, they may refrain from doing it in the future. If your friend confides in you, help them get help so the problem goes away. If necessary, confide in an adult you trust.

### 2. Ignore them

If there is an isolated incident where you are being bullied, don't respond to the instigator. Cyberbullies who do not get a response from their target may just move on. They are looking for a response – don't give it to them!

### 3. Never retaliate

Be the bigger person and never retaliate against a cyberbully. Retaliation only further perpetuates the cycle of violence, and does nothing to solve the problem. Plus, if you retaliate you could get into trouble for what you are doing or saying to them!

### 4. Tell them to stop

For repeated bullying, if ignoring the bully doesn't work, tell them to stop. Let them know that what they are doing is hurtful and, more importantly, lame and uncool. Be respectful in approaching them and never come off in an aggressive manner.

### 5. Talk about it

Tell someone if you're the target of cyberbullying. Whether it's your parents, a teacher, or another trusted adult, or even your best friend, never keep the fact that you're being bullied to yourself. We know it's not fun and it's hard to talk about it, but you should give others a chance to come through for you. It could help make the problem go away, which is the ultimate goal.

### 6. Save the evidence

Record all instances of cyberbullying. Print out Facebook messages and emails, save text messages, and capture screen shots when cyberbullying occurs. Then turn these documents over to an adult who you believe can help.

### 7. Block access to cyberbullies

Block cyberbullies from contacting you. Most websites and software programs have the ability for you to block certain users from messaging you or even being able to 'see' you online. Newer phones have the capability to block preset phone numbers, and you can also contact your cell phone service provider (for example, AT&T or Verizon) to help. If certain people simply cannot reach you, it will be more difficult for them to bully you.

### 8. Report it to the content provider

If you don't know who the cyberbully is, contact the content provider of the site where the cyberbullying is occurring and make a report. The most popular web sites (like Facebook, YouTube and Google) make it pretty easy to report cyberbullying. Harassment is a violation of the terms of service of all reputable web sites.

### 9. Never pass along messages from cyberbullies

If you receive a hurtful or embarrassing messages or photos of someone else, delete it and refrain from forwarding it to others. Don't be part of the problem, be part of the solution. You can stop cyberbullying by letting your friends know that it simply isn't cool.

### 10. Call the police

If you feel your safety (or the safety of someone else) is in danger, call the police immediately. Any time there is a threat, tell an adult. They can help you make sure that your safety is protected.

*January 2012*

⇨ The above information is reprinted with kind permission from the Cyberbullying Research Center. Visit their website www.cyberbullying.usfor further information.

*© 2012 Cyberbullying Research Center*

# Key Facts

- 44% of suicides among 10- to 14-year-olds may be bullying related. (page 4)

- Over 20% of children admit to being a bully or participating in bully-like activities. (page 4)

- On a daily average 160,000 children miss school because they fear they will be bullied if they attend classes. (page 4)

- On a monthly average 282,000 students are physically attacked by a bully each month. (page 4)

- A child commits suicide as a direct result of being bullied once every half hour. (page 4)

- Two-thirds (66%) of 1,010 parents of children aged eight to 16 polled say they witness different forms of mental intimidation while watching their children play sport. Teasing (43%), swearing (40%), taunts (34%) and verbal threats (16%) are common tactics of the sports bullies. (page 7)

- Children as young as eight are victims of mental and physical bullying on the school playing field, according to research published today by Marylebone Cricket Club (MCC) and Chance to Shine. (page 7)

- According to Bullying UK's 2006 National Bullying Survey, 69% of children in the UK report being bullied. (page 8)

- Why are people bullied? 40% say it's because of 'looks', 25% say it is because they are 'good at something', 10% attribute bullying to their race, 8% SEN/Health, 5% religion and 3% sexuality. (page 8)

- 25% of children who are persistently bullied say they have changed their personality. (page 8)

- Both bullies and their victims have been found to be three times more likely to consider suicide or actions of self-harm by the age of 11, according to recent research conducted by the University. (page 9)

- Suicide is a leading cause of death in the UK; in 2008 there were 4,282 recorded suicides in England alone. Men between the ages of 15 and 24 are at a particularly high risk. (page 9)

- Racist bullying is the only type of bullying that schools have a duty to record. (page 11)

- Alarmingly, more than half of gay young people say they're homophobically bullied, one in six saying they've been physically abused. And 6% have received death threats. (page 12)

- More than four in five gay pupils say homophobic language distresses them. In schools where such language is never challenged, the rate of homophobic bullying stands at 68% – compared with 37% in schools where homophobic language is always challenged. (page 13)

- Over 50% of pupils have frequently heard anti-gay remarks being made in schools. (page 13)

- Around 16 pupils in the UK kill themselves every year due to the distress over bullying. (page 21)

- Britons are among the world's most bullied workers, with seven in 10 admitting to being bullied by bosses or colleagues … our European counterparts also suffer badly … with a staggering 83% claiming to be victims. This compares to 65% of bullied Americans and 55% of harassed Asian workers. (page 23)

- Making offensive calls is actually a criminal offence. Anyone who is found guilty could have to pay a large fine. They may also be given a six-month prison sentence. (page 29)

- Almost one in five young people in the UK have been the victim of cyber-bullying, according to research carried out by academics at Anglia Ruskin University. (page 30)

- Bullying, and having been bullied online mostly go hand in hand. Around 60% of those who bully have been bullied by others. (page 31)

- The social network of choice for most pupils levelling abuse at their teachers was Facebook (77%), while 21% used RateMyTeachers.com, 6% used Twitter and 1% used MySpace. (page 35)

- 46% of teachers surveyed for Becta's E-Safety and Web 2.0 report, reported negative experiences caused by pupils using web 2.0 technologies. (page 35)

## Act of Communications 2003

The Communications Act 2003 governs the Internet, e-mail, mobile phone calls and text messaging. This means that it is an offence to send messages or other matter that are 'grossly offensive or of an indecent, obscene or menacing character', whether the targeted person actually sees the message or not.

## Bullying

A form of aggressive behaviour used to intimidate someone. It can be inflected both physically and mentally (psychologically).

## Communications Act

The Communications Act 2003 governs the internet, email, mobile phone calls and text messaging. Under section 127 of the act it is an offence to send messages that are 'grossly offensive or of an indecent, obscene or menacing character', and the offence occurs whether those targeted actually receive the message or not.

## Cyberbullying

Cyberbullying is when technology is used to harass, embarrass or threaten to hurt someone. A lot is done through social networking sites such as Facebook, Twitter, MySpace and Bebo. Bullying via mobile phones is also a form of cyberbullying. With the use of technology on the rise, there are more and more incidents of cyberbullying.

## Discrimination

Unfair treatment against someone because of the group/class they belong too.

## Harassment

Usually persistent (but not always), a behaviour that is intended to cause distress and offence. It can occur on the school playground, in the workplace and even at home.

## Homophobic bullying

Homophobia is the fear or hatred of people who are attracted to the same sex as themselves (e.g. disliking lesbians, gay men and bisexuals). This form of bullying is slightly different because of the personal motivation that drives it, in this case being directed at someone who is gay, lesbian or thought to be by others.

## Non-verbal abuse

Can be thought of as a kind of 'psychological warfare' because instead of using spoken words or direct physical violent behaviour, this form of abuse involves the use of mimicry (teasing someone by mimicking them), offensive gestures or body language.

## Racist bullying

Targeting a person because of their race, colour or beliefs. There is a difference between racism and racial harassment: racial harassment refers to words and actions that are intentionally said/done to make the target feel small and degraded due to their race or ethnicity.

## Troll / Troller

Troll is Internet slang for someone who intentional posts something online to provoke a reaction. The idea behind the trolling phenomenon is that it is about humour, mischief, and some argue, freedom of speech; it can be anything from a cheeky remark to a violent threat. However, sometimes these internet pranks can be taken too far, such as a person who defaces Internet tributes site, causing the victims family further grief.

## Verbal abuse

Spoken words out loud intended to cause harm, such as suggestive remarks, jokes or name calling.

# Assignments

The following tasks have been designed to help you think through the debate surrounding bullying in our society and provide a better understanding of the topic.

**1.** Imagine you are an Agony Aunt (or Uncle) writing for a national newspaper. A young girl has written in admitting that she is being bullied at school and is miserable. Write a suitable reply giving advice and information on where she may look for support in order to tackle her concerns. Read the article Agony Aunt letters on page 17 for inspiration.

**2.** Read 'Victims of bullying' and 'University discovers link between bullying, self-harm and suicide on pages 8 and 9. Using these articles, pretend you are writing a summary for your local newspaper about how bullying affects young people today.

**3.** 'Calling someone names doesn't hurt them as much as hitting them.' Discuss this statement in small groups and feed back to your class.

**4.** Unchallenged homophobic language is so ingrained in everyday language that even the word 'gay' has come to be used when referring to anything worthless or without value. Talk about words which form part of a homophobic bully's vocabulary. What images do they bring to mind? Why are they so harmful? What do you think schools can do to combat the use of this language?

**5.** Homophobic bullying doesn't just happen in schools, it also occurs in the workplace. Design a poster that could be used in both schools and offices to highlight this harmful behaviour, and offer advice and help to someone who might be a victim.

**6.** You see a boy at your school being bullied, but he refuses to tell anyone. He thinks that by telling his parents or a teacher the situation will get worse. You really want to help him, but you are worried about the backlash from the bully if they find out. What do you do? Discuss with a partner.

**7.** Find a partner and roleplay an incident of bullying, with one of you being the bully and the other the victim. Each take turns playing the bully and the victim. How did you feel playing each role? How do you think the other person felt? How do you think the situation could be diffused?

**8.** Image that you are the manager of a small company and you are giving a talk about workplace bullying. Give a speech to your employees explaining what you consider to be bullying behaviour, how you intend to tackle the problem and what the consequences of bullying would be. Use the article 'Britons are the world's most bullied workers, study reveals' on page 23 and 'Root causes of bullying behaviour in the workplace' on page 24 as a starting point.

**9.** What types of technology might be used to bully someone? Create a list and then address each item in turn and find ways of how to protect yourself and keep safe whilst using that technological device.

**10.** Design an app that will educate Internet users about cyberbullying, especially in relation to social networking sites and how to keep safe online.

**11.** Research the CyberMentors initiative by Beatbullying at www.cybermentors.org.uk. The site uses a range of interactive features, such as online chat and videos. Write a review of the website, focussing on how effective you think the initiate will be in tackling cyberbullying and how engaging you think the site is for young people.

**12.** Visit The Trolling Academy (www.trollingacademy. org). What is trolling? What are all the different types of 'troll'? And how can you handle and deal with trolling?

**13.** Olympic diver Tom Daley was the victim of abusive messages sent via Twitter. 17-year old Reece Messer was arrested on suspicion of malicious communication and was issued with a harassment warning. Police held Messer under the Malicious Communications Act, which came into force in 1988. Research some other high profile media cases where someone was the victim of online abuse. What happened? What laws were the perpetrators charged with breaking? What effect did the incident have on society?

**14.** Research more about the Act of Communications 2003 and also the Malicious Communications Act: what are they? How do they keep you safe? What other laws are there to keep you safe from cyberbullying?

**15.** Design a leaflet that will be handed out in schools, explaining how to change the privacy settings of your Facebook profile. What the different settings mean and what dangers could be encountered by having a public profile.

**16.** Watch the 2010 film The Karate Kid, starring Jaden Smith. Write a report discussing how the film highlights the issue of bullying.

# Acknowledgements

The publisher is grateful for permission to reproduce the following material.

While every care has been taken to trace and acknowledge copyright, the publisher tenders its apology for any accidental infringement or where copyright has proved untraceable. The publisher would be pleased to come to a suitable arrangement in any such case with the rightful owner.

### Chapter One: Understanding bullying

*Bullying,* © Government of South Australia, *Bullying statistics,* © 2012 Cait, *As Kate Middleton knows, girls make the best bullies,* © Telegraph Media Group Limited 2012, *Teasing, taunts and threats: school-children are waging 'psychological warfare' on the nation's playing fields,* © 2011 Cricket Foundation Enterprises, *Victims of bullying,* © 2012 Crown copyright, *University discovers link between bullying, self-harm and suicide,* © 2012 Jack Shardlow, The Boar, *Racist bullying,* © 2012 Ealing, *Advice to resolve racist bullying,* © Family Lives, *What is homophobic bullying?,* © EACH 2012 Ltd, *The curse of homophobic bullying,* © 2012 Press Association, *Since when was racist bullying the only 'wrong' form of bullying?,* © Telegraph Media Group Limited 2012, *Ten things you can do to challenge homophobia,* © EACH 2012 Ltd, *Have you been bullied for having red hair?,* © 2012 Everything for Redheads, *Agony Aunt letters,* © 2012 Christina Hughes, *What to do about bullying,* © Crown copyright, *Face bullying with confidence,* © 2011 Kidpower Teenpower Fullpower International, *If you are a bully...,* © Family Lives, *Britons are the world's most bullied workers, study reveals,* © 2012 AOL (UK) Limited, *Root causes of bullying behaviour (workplace),* © Chartered Management Institute 2012, *Bullying in the workplace,* © ACAS 2012, Euston Tower, 286 Euston Road, London NW1 3JJ.

### Chapter Two: Cyberbullying

*Cyberbullying – an introduction,* © Crown copyright is reproduced with the permission of Her Majesty's Stationery Office, *Cyberbullying,* © Government of South Australia, *Bullying on social networks,* © Crown copyright, *Bullying on mobile phones,* © Crown copyright, *Cyberbullying affects one in five youngsters in UK,* © 2012 Anglia Ruskin University, *EU Kids Online – bullying summary,* © UKCCIS Evidence Group, *The 12 types of Internet troller,*

© The Crocels Trolling Academy, *What is trolling? And why do people do it?,* © 2010 Wirral Council, *Teachers report widespread cyberbullying by pupils and parents,* © Guardian News & Media Ltd 2012, *Cyberbullying – Supporting school staff,* © 2012 Association of Teachers and Lecturers, *Tweeter jailed for racist abuse,* © 2004–2012 SquareDigital Media Ltd, *Cheryl Cole reveals Internet bullying hell: 'people say I look fat',* © 2012 AOL (UK) Limited, *Responding to cyberbullying,* © 2012 Cyberbullying Research Center.

### Illustrations:

Pages 20, 31: Don Hatcher; pages 11, 22: Simon Kneebone; pages 18, 33: Angelo Madrid.

### Images:

Cover and pages i, 30: © nautilus_shell_studios; page 5: © Christopher Futcher; page 9: © Jackie Staines; page 14: © Katerine Evans; page 16: © Caroline Hoos; page 27: © leeavision; page 32: © Paul Pantazescu; page 36: © Peter Booth; page 41: © Micah Burke.

### Additional acknowledgements:

Editorial on behalf of Independence Educational Publishers by Cara Acred. Layout by Jackie Staines.

With thanks to the Independence team: Mary Chapman, Sandra Dennis, Christina Hughes, Jan Sunderland and Amy Watson.

Cara Acred

Cambridge

September, 2012